MasterStress

A professional resource for assessing and managing stress

Dr Roy Bailey

Speechmark

Published by
Speechmark Publishing Ltd, 70 Alston Drive, Bradwell Abbey, Milton Keynes MK13 9HG, United Kingdom
Tel: +44 (0) 1908 326944 Fax: +44 (0) 1908 326960

www.speechmark.net

002-5647 Printed in the United Kingdom by CMP (UK) Ltd

British Library cataloguing in publication data
Bailey, Roy Victor
MasterStress : a professional resource for assessing and managing stress.
1. Stress management. 2. Stress (Psychology)—Testing.
I. Title
616.9'8–dc22

ISBN 978 0 86388 759 8

FSC MIX Paper FSC® C004309

Contents

Introduction

Who is this resource for?

MasterStress has been designed for busy practitioners who require a professional and practical resource to assist them in helping their clients to (1) understand stress, (2) identify stress, and (3) better manage the stress in their lives and their relationships.

How to use *MasterStress*

MasterStress is arranged in a format that is both easy to use and clear to follow. It is suitable for work with both individual clients and groups. Part 1 'The knowledge base' outlines definitions of stress and describes the *MasterStress* model of stress regulation. Practitioners can use this section to assist those people who prefer to have a conceptual understanding of stress and an appreciation of the underlying model of stress regulation before engaging with the *MasterStress* activities in Part 2.

Those clients who want to do something practical straight away to better understand and identify stress, and to manage their own stress, can miss out Part 1 and go straight on to the activities.

In Part 2 the purpose of each activity is outlined, the resources required are listed and there is a full explanation of how the activity should be conducted. Together the activities form a comprehensive set of stress assessment and stress management interventions that can be used with both individuals and groups.

Each activity can be used singly or in combination with others: for example, you could use a combination of activities that identify sources of stress and the stress experienced by a client or group of clients as a baseline before going on to select one of the stress management interventions. After practising the interventions, you could then reassess the client or group by once again evaluating any sources of stress and the degree of stress they experience after the intervention. This is just one way in which you can use the *MasterStress* activities. However, you should feel free to experiment with different individual, or combinations of, activities that are most appropriate for the people with whom you work.

Materials

The *MasterStress* activities can be used in a range of ways to assist each client. Many professional psychologists, coaches, counsellors and therapists are likely to be using similar materials with their clients. For those already experienced in empowering clients to assess and better manage stress, it is useful to summarise the main types of materials that have been shown to contribute to client learning. Those new to the field should find using selected resources along with the *MasterStress* activities a helpful assistant in their work.

Marker pens and pencils

Keep plenty of pens and pencils available: marker pens, highlighter pens, gel pens and ballpoints. They are useful for emphasising learning points and may be needed at any time during an activity. Not having a supply of pens and pencils can make it difficult for the professional and the client to track and record their activities.

Overhead projector

Having ready access to an overhead projector is particularly helpful if you are running any of the activities with groups. An overhead projector provides a focal point and serves to direct attention to any points you are making. Typically, overhead projectors are useful for bullet-pointing key issues such as definitions of stress, sources of threat and stress, and examples of adaptive and maladaptive coping.

Flip chart

Key issues can be listed on a flip chart. In addition, using a flip chart allows the professional to work in a highly flexible way with individuals and groups. Client concerns that are sometimes lost in discussion can be captured on a flip chart. Keeping a record on a flip chart avoids the potential loss of significant client information, and this is especially important over a series of sessions. The sensitive use of flip charts with the activities can nicely convey the character of clients' concerns about stress and their management of stress.

Notepads and personal journals

A notepad is useful to clients as a quick reference reminder of significant points that may be raised during a stress assessment or stress management activity. It is valuable for clients to have their own handwritten notes as well as any that may be provided by the professional.

Personal journals are, of course, confidential. However, clients may wish to share the information in their personal journals with the psychologist, counsellor, coach or therapist with whom they are working.

The use of notebooks and personal journals with clients is essential if you are working with a client over weeks or months as they will help to refresh the client's memory. They can also be used to monitor the progress clients are making over a period of time in better managing their stress.

Digital audio and computer technology

Clients may find it useful to use computer technology such as a laptop or an electronic notebook as an adjunct to the *MasterStress* activities. These can be enlisted to make quick notes and bullet points that can be referred to later and printed out or elaborated on. They can also be used as electronic personal learning journals. A great advantage of using a laptop or electronic notebook is that clients can follow up their *MasterStress* activities by visiting key websites such as **www.speechmark.com** and **www.stresscabin.com** for further ways of managing personal and relationship stress.

Part 1 The knowledge base

The meaning of stress

Understanding stress provides us with the bedrock on which we can help people to identify stress and better manage and regulate the stress they may experience. A first step in this direction is being clear about what the concept of stress means. Defining it will make us aware of the assumptions we hold about stress and its management. Defining it also helps us to overcome confusions that might arise in our understanding of stress. By clarifying our understanding, we become clear about the way we explain the meaning of stress to the people and groups with whom we work.

Stress as a stimulus or external event

We have all experienced stress at some stage in our lives and this means that we all have an understanding of what it is. We have to qualify this, though. What we really mean is that we know what stress means *to us*. It follows from this that stress can mean different things to different people and, as a result, the concept of stress has given rise to a wide diversity of definitions. As practitioners helping people to understand, regulate and better manage their stress, we have to be clear about its meaning. The *Oxford Dictionary* (2005) defines stress as 'a state of mental or emotional strain resulting from adverse or demanding circumstances'. But stress has also been described as 'mental fatigue' (Bills, 1934), 'unusual demand' (Crawford, 1961), 'stressful situation' (Grinker & Spiegel, 1945), 'overload/underload' (Franklenhauser, 1976), 'stimulation underload' (Franklenhauser, 1974), 'role load', 'role conflict', 'role ambiguity' and 'role responsibility' (Kahn & Quinn, 1970). All of these definitions construe stress as something *external* to the person (or object); in short, stress is thought to be 'out there'. Unfortunately for stimulus definitions of stress, not everything 'out there' is stressful for everyone.

Stress as a response

Some experts have proposed *response*-based definitions of stress, suggesting that stress is best understood to be the *response state* of 'the total organism under extenuating circumstances' and not the result of an event or events in the external environment (Appley & Trumbull, 1967). One attractive definition of stress incorporates the notion of homeostasis – the principle of balance and equilibrium – in maintaining fundamental psychological and physiological functions. Stress is considered to be the 'strenuous effort to maintain essential functions at a required level' (Ruff & Korchin, 1964). However, it is not clear what these essential functions are, or the assumed 'required level' for psychosocial and physiological balance to be maintained. Also, this view of stress is circular: claiming that stress is strenuous effort is not saying much more than that stress is stress. A similar criticism can be levelled at the endocrinologist Hans Selye, often regarded as the 'father of stress', who defined stress as the 'non-specific response of the body to any demand made on it' (Selye, 1956). For Selye, stress was always a response to a stressor. Stressors are 'out there' in the environment. Typical stressors could be burns, excessive heat or cold, frustration with others, marital disagreements, combat fatigue and trauma.

The interactional view of stress

In his later work Selye foresaw the coming of the interactional view of stress (Selye, 1975). He noted that he was never inclined to define stress in terms of either stimulus or response; it arose as a result of an interaction. Richard Lazarus was the first psychologist to explicitly formulate that stress, and indeed coping, occurred as a result of individual cognitive transactions between the internal and external environments (Lazarus, 1966). Lazarus backed up his view of stress and coping with many experiments and provided an evidence-based approach to understanding them. The interactional view of stress and coping provides for a cognitive–behavioural model. It is cognitive because it contains the assumption that appraisal, thinking, memory and the meaning or significance of events for the individual experiencing them are the core mediators and causal agents in determining whether stress and coping occur. It is behavioural because it clearly incorporates how individuals go about trying to manage unwanted levels of personal stress.

The *MasterStress* approach to stress regulation

The approach to stress that I have developed takes the interactional understanding of stress and coping even further. In the *MasterStress* model, stress occurs when significant demands exceed the adaptive coping routines and skills adopted by the individual to regulate their emotions, thinking and behaviour. According to the model:

1 Stress occurs as a result of the interaction between a person and significant demands being made on them at any one time and over time.

2 Stress also assimilates the notion of coping.

3 This definition recognises that stress arises through difficulties in regulating our emotions and the demands made on us at any one time and over time. Importantly, it is the meaning or significance demands have for us, and whether we have a coping strategy available to us, that determines whether stress occurs.

In this sense, our *MasterStress* definition of stress gives rise to a stress regulation model of stress and coping. In this model some stress is good for us, but too much mobilises us to cope and take action to stem stress or deal with demanding situations we may face. Clearly, excessive and prolonged or chronic stress is bad for us and our relationships, and can lead to emotional, mental and physical health problems, in some cases resulting in stress disorders and a serious breakdown in mental and physical health.

The *MasterStress* model of stress regulation

The *MasterStress* model of stress regulation shows us how, as individuals, we make appraisals about the internal and external demands that are being made on us at any one time and over time. This is done through our cognitive evaluation of events. In the language of the model, this involves our primary and secondary appraisals of demands. Primary appraisals are concerned with whether we evaluate the demands made on us as benign, threatening or involving some form of harm or loss to ourselves or significant others.

If we appraise the demands being made on us as harmless, we can decide not to engage in coping or stress management. On the other hand, if we regard significant demands as being actually or potentially harmful to us, we can initiate secondary appraisals as to what coping strategies and stress management we can put into practice. We can then reappraise and re-evaluate whether our attempts at stress management have been 'successful' and helpful, or harmful to others or ourselves. The *MasterStress* model of stress

The *MasterStress* model of stress regulation

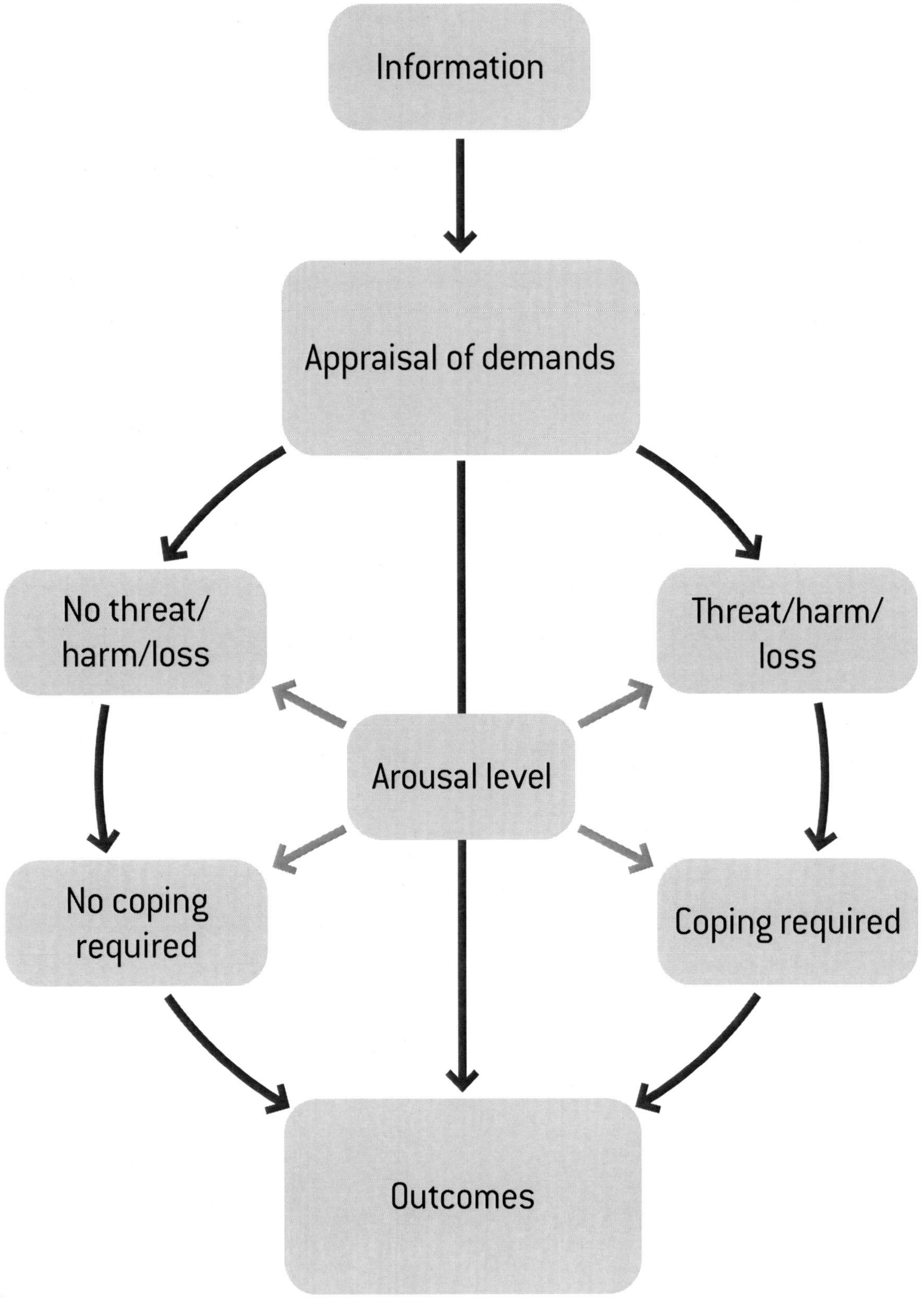

regulation does not guarantee that we will be free from the adverse effects of stress. Rather, it shows us how we can identify the sources of our stress and our coping choices, and how these can be changed if our coping and stress management lead to the removal of, or relief from, personal stress.

The model also accommodates the old adage that ‘to err is human’. We cannot always be certain that we have adopted the best coping strategy or stress management, or put into practice the ‘right’ choice to overcome the stress we may experience. Indeed, we may try to master stress by choosing maladaptive coping such as engaging in excessive alcohol consumption or hard drugs. However, the whole purpose of our primary and secondary appraisals is to assist us in our efforts to identify and better regulate any personal stress associated with significant demands being made on us at any one time and over time.

The *MasterStress* model of stress regulation helps us to map out the potential as well as the actual deleterious effects stress can have on our mental, emotional and physical health, and how well we are doing at regulating it and managing ourselves and our relationships with others.

Competence to practise *MasterStress* activities

Qualified practitioner psychologists, counsellors and therapists who are already experienced and competent in assessing and applying stress management interventions with people will be familiar with the time involved in planning and carrying out stress management and therapeutic sessions. However, those newer to the field of understanding, assessing and managing stress in others will find that the *MasterStress* activities each take 30–50 minutes to complete.
The activities are flexible and can therefore usefully be combined with other therapeutic psychological interventions.

Consistent with best practice, I would advise anyone who is not experienced or qualified in understanding, assessing and managing stress to carry out the *MasterStress* activities under the supervision of an appropriate professional such as a registered practitioner psychologist.

Part 2 *MasterStress* activities

Activity 1 The meaning of stress

PURPOSE

Clients should have a clear understanding of stress and what it means to them. Understanding the meaning of stress provides a sound knowledge base and this is important because understanding can help people take action to better manage stress in their relationships and in their personal and working lives.

RESOURCE

'The meaning of stress' chart

WHAT TO DO

1 Explain to the clients that you are going to examine and arrive at a clear understanding of important questions about stress. Everyone has something to say about stress.

2 Ask the following questions:

- What is stress?
- What forms does it take?
- How does it arise?
- How does it affect us?
- What can it do to us and our relationships?
- What can be done about stress?
- What benefits can we expect from better managing our stress?
- Who should help?
- What comes into *your* mind when you think of stress?

3 Brainstorm for up to 10 minutes and record everyone's contributions about stress on a flip chart.

4 Write up the conclusions on large sheets of paper and pin them up for everyone to see.

5 Invite comments and ask for clarification if necessary.

6 What have the clients learned about stress from this part of the exercise? Discuss this fully and invite each person to write it on their copy of the 'meaning of stress' chart.

The meaning of stress

POINTS TO SHARE

Stress covers a wide range of views, thoughts, feelings, body conditions, health and behaviour.

Stress is a complex phenomenon.

Stress is a general framework for better understanding disruption to health and well-being.

Stress is usually regarded as unpleasant, undesirable and unwanted, although this need not always be the case.

Stress is at the root of many common concerns, for example anxiety, anger, depression, colds, headaches, boredom, absenteeism.

Stress can be highly individual: 'one person's meat is another's poison'.

Stress issues can be causes or effects of stress: for example, role conflict, role load and role ambiguity are strictly speaking 'causes', whereas frustration, anger, anxiety and fatigue are 'effects'.

Stress occurs when significant internal or external demands are experienced as exceeding a person's available personal, social and/or collective resources.

SUMMARY

We all know something about stress. It is a common condition, not always bad, but usually unwanted, unpleasant and undesirable. It can, and often does, undermine people's health, personal well-being and family relationships. Stress is also individual, showing up in particular ways for each person.

Activity 2 **Assessing stressful behaviour**

PURPOSE

Managing stress should not be restricted to just talking about it in the training room, stress-counselling session or therapy clinic. These are good places for getting self-reports from clients about their problems, and self-reports are essential building blocks in the process of effective stress management. Sometimes clients may also overtly display some of the difficulties they say they are experiencing. However, this tells us little about the *actual* occurrences of stress and how these behaviours are expressed by people in their daily lives. You need to have valid information about stress *as it happens* as well as about those times when clients are free from stressful behaviours.

RESOURCE

Stressful behaviour record

WHAT TO DO

1 Once sufficient rapport has been established, explain to the client the purpose of recording stressful behaviour.

2 Explain that stressful behaviour happens in *time*, *space* and *place*. Tell them that you need to know *when* their specific stressful behaviours occur, *who* and/or *what* is present and *where* these behaviours take place.

3 Make it clear to the client that they need to know the pattern of their stressful behaviour. Point out that stressful behaviour usually has a sequence, but it will be unique to each person.

4 Check that they have understood you so far and answer any questions they might put to you.

5 At about this time introduce the 'stressful behaviour record', discuss it and decide on the following points:

- What specific thinking, feeling and behaving will be recorded?
- Who will make and keep the observation records?
- What will be the duration of the observation period?
- What form should the observation take?
- When should you meet again to review/assess the results?

6 When you meet again, look for patterns of stress and consider how these relate to what you have found out from the observations the client has listed on the stressful behaviour record.

7 Share and discuss the results and the analysis of the stressful behaviour record. Questions to explore are:

- *What* does their stressful behaviour suggest to the client?
- *How* does the record illustrate the kind of stress they are experiencing?
- *What* is the *pattern* of their stressful behaviour?
- *When* is stress particularly a problem for them?

---

8 With the help of the client, draw up a list of salient points that they can learn from their observations on the stressful behaviour record.

---

9 Examine these further questions with them:

- What further observations are needed using the stressful behaviour record?
- What further observations, if any, are required using a different method of recording stressful behaviour?
- Have enough observations been made?
- Do you and/or the client know enough about their stressful behaviour to begin considering a stress management strategy?

---

10 Make a summary of the observations on the stressful behaviour record, saying what you have learned and what future actions the client may or may not take to better manage their stress.

Stressful behaviour record

Name

Date

Description of behaviour

What happened

Where

When

Who/with whom

Duration

Assessor

Activity 3 **The TFB model of stressful behaviour**

PURPOSE

People can become confused and worried about the stress they are experiencing in their lives. They often want to know *why* they are suffering from so much stress. A useful approach to this question is to explain to them that their stress arises out of the way they are thinking, feeling and behaving (TFB).

This activity provides a useful framework within which stress can be understood. It is useful in three ways. It helps to reassure people that their stress *can be understood* and is *understandable*. It makes it possible to analyse stress within a given set of parameters or boundaries. Perhaps most important of all, it helps to indicate what areas of thinking, feeling and behaving might need changing if the person is to have less stress in their life.

RESOURCES

TFB model of stressful behaviour
TFB example

WHAT TO DO

1 Introduce the 'TFB model of stressful behaviour' and invite the client to look at it with you. Give examples and explain that stressful behaviour does not just happen; it comes about through people's:

- Thinking
- Feeling
- Behaving.

Tell the client that you sometimes call this the TFB model of stressful behaviour.

2 Take some time to go over the TFB model and ensure that the client understands it. Clarify any misunderstandings or confusions that arise.

3 Present the 'TFB example' (or one of your own) to enhance your explanation of the model.

4 Point out that the model is interactive and that people's thinking affects their feelings and behaviour and their behaviour can affect their feelings and thinking.

5 Explore with the client the way they are thinking, feeling and behaving, and what they say when they are experiencing too much stress.

6 Now explore how they are thinking, feeling and behaving on those occasions when stress is *not* a problem for them.

---

7 Map out and show the relationship between the client's thinking, feeling and behaviour, using the TFB model of stressful behaviour, and discuss it with them.

---

8 Come to a shared understanding of the model and the way the client is thinking, feeling and behaving during times of too much stress and times when they are stress-free.

---

9 Now work out with the client what *specific kinds* of thinking, feeling and behaving create more or less stress for them.

---

10 Ask them to write this down in the 'Personal notes' following the illustration of the TFB model.

---

11 Invite the client to take a few moments to reflect on what they have discovered about their different ways of thinking, feeling and behaving that lead them to experience more or less stress.
What do they and you have to say about the stress in their lives? What might need to be changed?
What needs to be kept the same?

TFB model of stressful behaviour

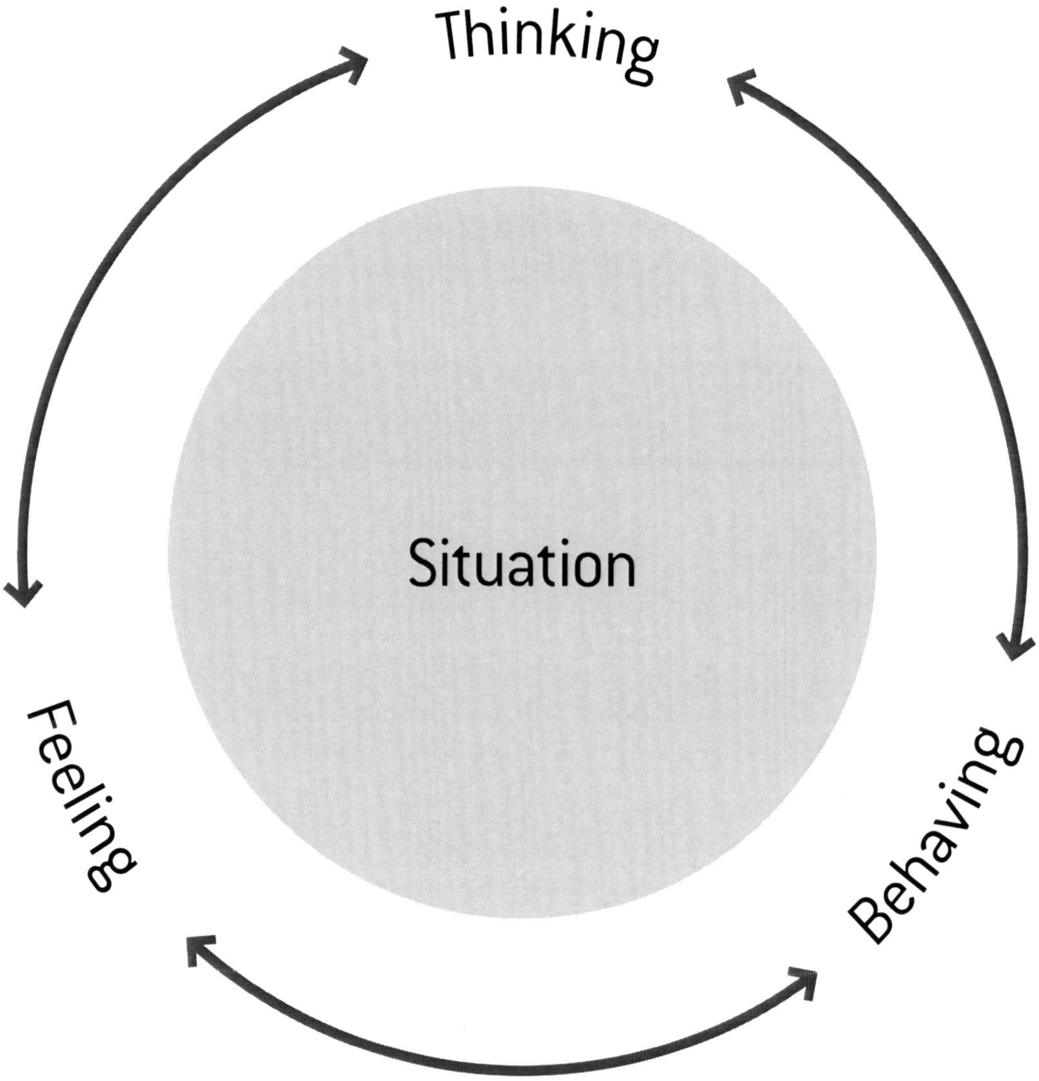

Personal notes

TFB example

Thinking

He/she is not interested in me

I have nothing useful to say/contribute

I am dull and boring

People like me get embarrassed easily

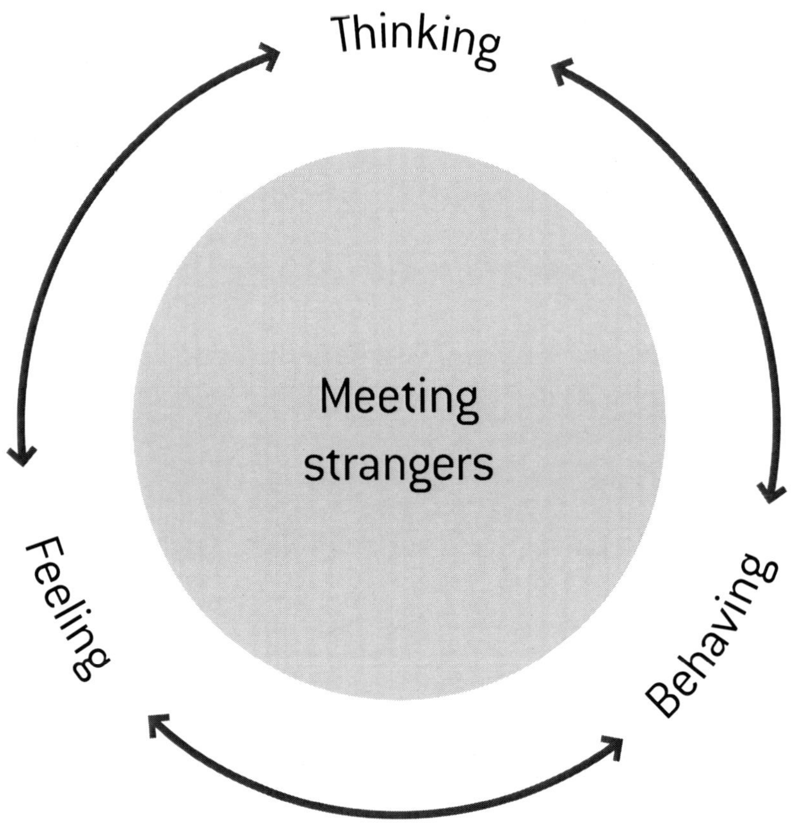

Feeling

Heart racing,

palms sweating,

lump in throat,

going hot and cold

Behaving

Saying sorry,

apologising for not being good at talking to/ meeting people,

looking away and staring into space

Activity 4 **Stress arousal**

PURPOSE

When people are experiencing stress they sometimes describe themselves as feeling tense or 'all coiled up' inside. Others may say their muscles feel tight or that they feel like a pressure cooker ready to blow up at any moment. There are many other descriptions people give to the stress they say they experience. They may be different, but they are all valid in their own way.

Common to all the descriptions of stress people give is 'stress arousal'. Stress arousal refers to a person's perceived level of the physiological activity taking place inside their body at any one time.

Stress arousal is essential to all human beings – they need it to survive – but not too much of it. Too much or too little stress arousal impairs performance on tasks and can damage personal relationships.

RESOURCES

Stress arousal curve
Stress arousal audit

WHAT TO DO

1 Explain that stress is closely associated with what we call 'stress arousal'. Simplify your explanation by saying something like,

> Stress arousal is an indicator of the amount of physiological activity going on inside your body or system; too much stress arousal and too little stress arousal can interfere with:
>
> - your performance on tasks
> - how well you think and concentrate
> - how much control you have over your behaviour
> - the way you feel about yourself
> - how you behave towards others.

2 Show the client the 'stress arousal curve', discuss it with them and ask them to compare the way in which too much or too little stress arousal can affect their thinking, feelings and behaviour.

3 Explain that too little stress arousal is called 'under-arousal' and too much stress arousal 'over-arousal'.

4 Make clear that different levels of personal stress arousal will affect the client's performance on tasks and how they relate to other people.

5 Ask the client where they perceive themselves to be on the stress arousal curve *right at this very moment*. Then ask them to make a cross on the curve to show where they perceive themselves to be on it.

6 Ask them to do the same for where they perceive themselves to be on the stress arousal curve *most of the time* and mark it with a circle.

7 Identify with the client any *specific* stress problem they are trying to resolve. Help them to work out their level of arousal and again ask them to record it on the stress arousal curve.

8 Compare and discuss with the client the results on their copy of the curve, how close or far apart they are and their similarities and differences. What are the results like in the morning, at midday, in the afternoon and in the evening?

9 Where and when are the best and worst points for them?

10 Invite the client to *discover* and *decide* if they are mostly over- or under-aroused, or near their *optimal* arousal on the stress arousal curve, at work, at home, during the morning, at midday, in the afternoon or at night.

11 You can assess a broader range of situations with this approach by introducing the 'stress arousal audit'.

12 Invite the client to *record* and *review* with you those situations where their stress arousal falls into the optimum band for them and where they are performing well. Discuss this with them and compare it with those *contexts*, *settings* and *times* where they are under-aroused or over-aroused and are under-performing in their relationships at home or at work.

13 Come to an agreed view with the client on the situations and levels of stress arousal affecting them.

14 Ask them to write a brief description of this view, read it back to you and tell you what they think it means.

Stress arousal curve

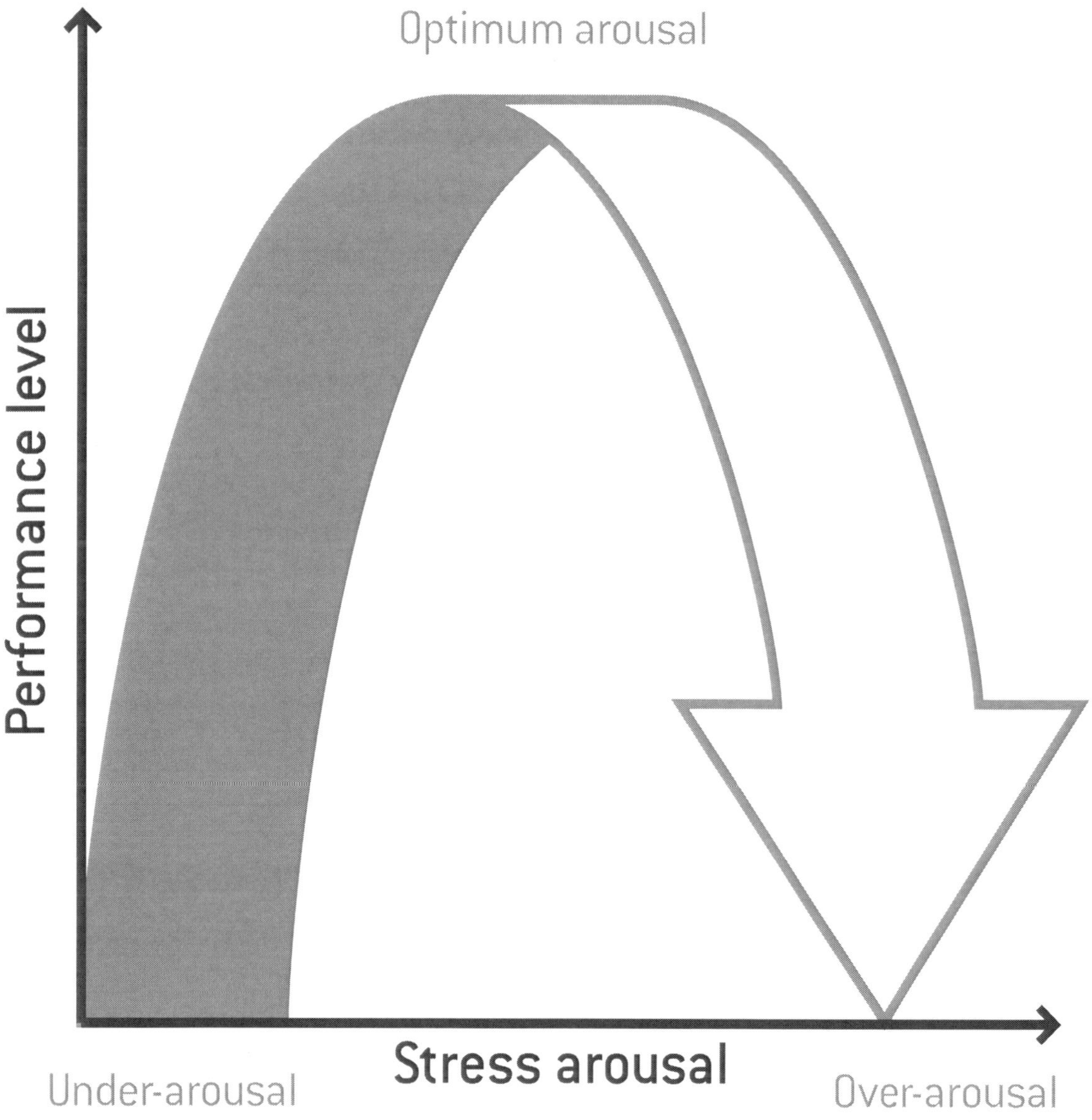

Stress arousal audit

Please complete this personal audit for the stressful situations you are facing. Record a brief description of the situation and the degree of stress arousal you experience. If your stress arousal is 'too low' circle 1, if it is 'about right' circle 2, and if it is 'too high' circle 3.

Situation

A

1 2 3

B

1 2 3

C

1 2 3

D

1 2 3

E

1 2 3

Additional observations

Name

Date

Activity 5 **Stressful situations**

PURPOSE

Sometimes it is necessary to identify and establish the specific situations that are stressful to clients. It is also helpful to get an idea of what particular forms of stress are the most typical. For example, in the workplace managers and other staff need to know what situations are stressful for them, the stress they experience and who is involved in these situations.

RESOURCE

Stressful situations inventory

WHAT TO DO

1 Say to the clients 'I find "X" stressful. What is stressful for you?'

2 Ask them to carry out the following steps:

- Pair with another person and identify what is stressful for each of you.
- Now complete the 'stressful situations inventory'.
- Describe as many relevant situations as you can.
- Be as specific as you can.
- Share, compare and discuss your findings.
- Feed back to each other what you have learned about situations that you and the other person find stressful.
- Summarise and put the situations into rank order. Show the most stressful as Rank 1, the next as Rank 2, then Rank 3, and so on.

3 Explain to the clients that assessing their stressful situations can:

- increase their awareness of their pattern of personal stress
- identify specific situations they can work on to reduce stress
- help them to explore ways to better manage stressful situations.

Stressful situations inventory

Description of episode

What happened?

Stress experienced

Who was involved?

Description of episode

What happened?

Stress experienced

Who was involved?

Description of episode

What happened?

Stress experienced

Who was involved?

Description of episode

What happened?

Stress experienced

Who was involved?

Description of episode

What happened?

Stress experienced

Who was involved?

Description of episode

What happened?

Stress experienced

Who was involved?

Activity 6 **Stress screening schedule**

PURPOSE

When a previously committed, enthusiastic and motivated person disengages from their relationships or their work, their stress level may be so extreme that it can lead to 'burnout'. Being able to recognise stress, especially in the early stages, can save the individual and other people from unnecessary suffering.

RESOURCE

Stress screening schedule

WHAT TO DO

1 Point out that stress can be present at any particular moment and can persist over longer periods of time.

2 When this happens people increase the risk of burnout. Burnout is a progressive form of stress that occurs over a period of time.

3 Point out that there are five main stress phases of burnout: enthusiasm, frustration, stagnation, withdrawal, isolation. These phases of stress progressively 'disable' the individual and can undermine their personal relationships.

4 Write up on a flip chart the five stress phases of burnout. Invite discussion with the client. Now assist them in completing the 'stress screening schedule'.

5 Summarise the responses given on the stress screening schedule.

6 Invite the client to say what features of stress they notice.

7 Ask if it is always easy to detect burnout in ourselves and other people.

Stress screening schedule

		Yes	No
1	Have you been drinking, smoking or eating more than usual?	☐	☐
2	Do you have difficulty sleeping at night?	☐	☐
3	Are you more 'touchy' and argumentative than usual?	☐	☐
4	Do you have trouble with your boss?	☐	☐
5	Have you or a loved one experienced a serious illness recently?	☐	☐
6	Have you recently separated or divorced?	☐	☐
7	Has there been an increase in marital or family arguments?	☐	☐
8	Have you been experiencing sexual difficulties?	☐	☐
9	Has a close relative or friend died recently?	☐	☐
10	Have you married recently or started living with someone?	☐	☐
11	Has there been a pregnancy or birth in your family?	☐	☐
12	Do you have financial problems?	☐	☐
13	Have you been dismissed from work or become unemployed?	☐	☐
14	Do you feel jumpy or on edge, or fly off the handle at little things?	☐	☐
15	Do you watch television for more than three hours a day?	☐	☐
16	Have you recently been in trouble with the law?	☐	☐
17	Has there been an increase in the number of deadlines you face or hours you work?	☐	☐
18	Have you recently moved or changed the place where you live?	☐	☐
19	Do you have trouble with your in-laws?	☐	☐
20	Are you exposed to constant noise at home or at work?	☐	☐
	Total	☐	☐

Name **Contact tel. no.**

Activity 7 Are you stress-prone?

PURPOSE

People have to cope with the many and varied demands made on them at work and in their personal lives. Some people find this more difficult than others. With this in mind it useful to be aware of how stress-prone clients may be and this can be discovered by identifying their typical behaviour pattern. If it is type 'A', they are stress-prone; if type 'B', they are less intense in their behaviour and not so stress-prone.

RESOURCE

Stress-prone scale questionnaire

WHAT TO DO

1 Ask the client to consider the following questions:

- What do we mean by a stress-prone personality?
- Is it the same as, say, being accident-prone?
- Under what circumstances might people be stress-prone? Is it a personality trait?
- How can we recognise a person who is stress-prone?

2 Elicit the client's views and ask them to write them up on a flip chart and display the sheets. Draw out the main issues. Explain that there is now good evidence from many psychological studies to show there is such a thing as being stress-prone. This is called the type A behaviour pattern and typical behaviour is:

- urgency of speech
- interrupting conversations
- always rushing to meet deadlines
- engaging in multiple tasks simultaneously, for example answering the telephone, talking to a colleague, writing a note
- preoccupation with work
- frequent restless body movements, for example pacing, twitching, mannerisms such as snorting, clearing the throat.

3 Write up the main characteristics on the flip chart and display the sheet.

4 Point out that there is also a type B behaviour pattern, which is the opposite of type A. Explain that type B is less intense, and someone with this behaviour pattern would:

- be more relaxed
- allow other people to finish what they are saying
- never rush
- carry out tasks sequentially
- have interests other than work
- be regarded as 'laid back'.

---

5 Ask the client to complete and score the 'stress-prone scale questionnaire' and then invite discussion. Suggested questions to facilitate the discussion are:

- What do these results suggest to you?
- Is there any pattern to them?
- What type are you? Why/why not?

Stress-prone scale questionnaire

Take your time in answering these questions. Please be as honest and open as possible. Discuss any statements you may be unclear about or that require further clarification. Put a tick in the box that applies to you.

Scoring guide Score 1 for every box ticked. Add all your scores and use the following categories to place your total score:

Cat. 1 = 3 points or less

Cat. 2 = 4–8 points

Cat. 3 = 9–13 points

Cat. 4 = 14 points or more.

		Yes
1	I feel there are not enough hours in the day to do all the things I must do.	☐
2	I always move, walk, talk and eat rapidly.	☐
3	I frequently feel impatient with the rate at which events take place.	☐
4	I unconsciously urge other people to 'get on with it' and hurry them up.	☐
5	I have a tendency to finish other people's sentences for them.	☐
6	I become unnecessarily irritated when the car in front of me goes at a pace that I consider too slow.	☐
7	I find it frustrating to wait in a queue (for example, waiting for a seat in a restaurant, waiting to pay at a filling station).	☐
8	I can't tolerate watching others perform tasks I know I can do faster.	☐
9	I often do more than one task at the same time (for example, I listen to colleagues while I am also on the phone and/or writing notes).	☐
10	I think about business or professional or personal problems when I am engaged in recreation.	☐
11	I become impatient when I have to do repetitive tasks (for example, mowing the lawn, dusting, sorting through junk mail, washing dishes).	☐
12	I rush through anything I read. If possible I obtain condensed summaries to save time.	☐
13	I have a tendency to vigorously emphasise key words in ordinary speech when there is no need to do so.	☐

Stress-prone scale questionnaire (cont.)

		Yes
14	I have a habit of expressing the last few words of my sentences far more rapidly than those at the beginning.	☐
15	I find it difficult not to bring the conversation around to my work and my interests.	☐
16	I pretend to listen to other people and their views when I am really preoccupied with my own thoughts.	☐
17	I frequently feel vaguely guilty when I relax and do nothing for a few hours or days.	☐
18	I attempt to fit in more and more in less and less time and as a result make few allowances for unforeseen occurrences.	☐
19	I frequently clench my fist, bang on the table or pound one fist into the palm of the other hand when making a conversational point.	☐
20	I find there are many deadlines in my job that are difficult to meet.	☐
21	I frequently clench my jaw.	☐
22	I find there are times when I grind my teeth.	☐
23	I frequently bring work home with me to do in the evening.	☐
24	I find I evaluate myself, other people and their activities more by numbers than before.	☐
25	I am satisfied with my present job.	☐
Total		☐

A person in category 4 is most stress-prone and can consider themselves significantly more at risk of heart disease. They require stress management and counselling. Persons in categories 2 and 3, although less likely to have heart disease than those in category 4, are still stress-prone and also require stress management and counselling. Generally, a category 1 person is least likely to have a heart attack and need not worry about being stress-prone.

Activity 8 Stress management interviewing

PURPOSE

As well as formulating a clear idea of what stress is and the kinds of stress clients are experiencing, it is useful to discover what they are doing to try to manage the stress in their lives.

Even though the attempts at managing their stress may not be successful, it helps to identify what clients are actually doing to cope with it, and the consequences of their coping efforts for themselves and others. It is therefore useful to provide them with a stress management interview structure. Within this structure they can safely explore:

1 the kinds of stress they are experiencing

2 the sources of their stress

3 the coping efforts they make to manage their stress

4 the consequences of their coping efforts.

Stress management interviewing allows you to work with clients towards an agreed view of their personal difficulties and a consideration of change they might want to make for the future.

RESOURCE

Stress management interview guide

WHAT TO DO

1 Explain that you will be conducting a stress management interview in this session.

2 Obtain the cooperation of the client and outline the structure of the interview. Emphasise that the aim is to gain a better understanding of the stress they are experiencing and what they do to manage it at present.

3 Check with the client that they understand the point of the session and invite questions if clarification is needed.

4 Tell the client that you are interested in their experience of stress, their ways of managing it and what results it has for them and others.

5 Introduce the 'stress management interview guide' and go over the main sections of it with the client.

6 Say something like,

> This interview is about the kinds of stress you are experiencing, where it comes from and how well you believe you are managing it right now.

7 Make sure the client feels safe enough to go through the interview with you and ensure that you will not be interrupted during the course of it.

8 Now go through the stress management interview guide. Ensure that each question is answered and in the client's own words and expressed in their own way. The questions need not be covered in sequential order. Make the interview as natural as possible. This may mean starting where the client needs to start. For example, if they wanted to start talking about the coping efforts they are making to manage stress, you would go to question 3 and work from there.

9 When the interview has been completed, briefly go over it again and ask if there is anything the client would like to amend or add to what they have told you.

10 Summarise the findings of the interview to the client, or ask them to do so and to say what changes, if any, they might need to consider making for the future.

Stress management interview guide

Name

Date of birth

Contact tel. no.

Interviewer Date

Reason for interview

Stress management interview guide (cont.)

1 What kinds of stress are you experiencing?

2 In your opinion, what are the sources of your stress and what gives rise to them?

3 What do you do to manage your stress and the demands made on you?

4 What short- and long-term effects, benefits or drawbacks does this have for your:

Self?

Associates/friends?

Family?

Working life/private life?

Stress management interview guide (cont.)

5 Would you say that on balance there is more stress in your life than you want. How do you know?

6 How satisfied/dissatisfied are you with your present way of coping? Why?

7 What changes, if any, would you be willing to make for the future?

Specifically, how/when/where will you change:

(a) the demands being made on you?

(b) the type of coping you put into practice?

8 Exactly what do you expect to be different for you and for others if you adopt this new way of coping?

Stress management interview guide (cont.)

9 How will you know if things have changed?

10 Summarise the demands made on you, the stress experienced, the coping efforts used, the outcome of your coping efforts, and how specifically you intend to change in the future.

Interviewer's notes

Activity 9 **Visual coping**

PURPOSE

Sometimes people do not have the words to describe how stressful life has been for them, or how they are trying to cope with stress. This may happen because the events and stress they experience are too overwhelming to put into words. Alternatively, some people may not be used to talking about the stress they experience or expressing themselves through spoken language.

Working with a visual approach to coping is often helpful for these people. Collage is an effective medium that encourages visual coping. People soon learn to use this method to *illustrate* their experiences of stress and the coping efforts they use to manage it. Interestingly, collage also helps people to talk more freely about themselves, their past and present difficulties and their future fears. As the adage suggests, 'a picture is worth a thousands words'. In stress management, a good collage makes it possible for the words to come to clients, allowing them to talk about coping with their stress.

RESOURCE

Visual coping guide

WHAT TO DO

1 Introduce the idea that people have many different ways of *expressing* the stress they experience and of coping with the demands being made on them at any one time.

2 Give a few examples of how people *express* the way they cope with stress, the stress they experience and the demands made on them, in time and over time. These can be from personal experience or examples of people the client knows about. If they find this difficult, use examples of personalities in the news or public figures in order to make the point clear.

3 Make the general point that everyone can *talk* about stress and how they might manage it better, but this may sometimes be difficult to do.

4 Explain to the client that if they feel this way, it may simply be because they are not used to talking to someone about their stress.

5 Check with them to see if *talking* about their stress would be too much for them at present. If this is the case, introduce them to the 'visual coping guide'.

6 Review with the client how, using pictorial representations of stress, the demands being made on them and how they cope can all be captured through collage.

7 Ensure that they understand why you are approaching stress management in this way with them, and reassure them by reminding them of the old adage 'a picture is worth a thousand words'.

8 Emphasise this point by also saying that collage can help the words come to them and make it easier for them to talk about their stress.

9 Ask the client to use three sheets of paper to make three separate but related collages covering (1) the demands they face, (2) the coping strategy they use, and (3) any stress they may be experiencing.

10 Brainstorm and then discuss possible ways in which the client could face the demands and how they could cope with the stress in their life. Use the collages to help the client talk about their stress problems and how they might go about changing the way they manage stress.

11 Finish by encouraging the client to make another collage that shows them successfully managing stress. Suggest that they hang it on the wall in a room where they can look at it daily to remind themselves that they have decided to change the way they will manage stress in the future.

Visual coping guide

The demands I face

•

The coping I use

•

The stress I experience

The demands I face

The coping I use

The stress I experience

Activity 10 **The art of reframing**

PURPOSE

The way people look at their situation in life affects how they feel. This is pertinent when you are working with clients to help them better manage the different kinds of stress they may be experiencing. Reframing involves helping people to perceive their difficulties and the context in which they occur in a different way.

A useful way of understanding this is to imagine that you have no knowledge of art or painting and see the same picture literally in different frames. A Van Gogh painting such as *Pavement Café at Night* might look like a mess of blues, greens and oranges seen in a cheap white plastic frame. Putting the same painting in a polished redwood frame with gold edging and a gold-plated title makes it look quite different. In an instant it becomes 'more valuable', simply because the frame it sits in has been changed.

There are many ways to use reframing with people. Use your imagination with clients and experiment with different kinds of reframing to help them manage their stress in more effective ways.

RESOURCES

Examples of reframing
Reframing schedule

WHAT TO DO

1 Explain that the way we see the problems and concerns in our lives is like having a particular frame of reference for each event. How we see or frame these events affects how we feel and whether or not we find an event stressful.

2 Make sure the client has understood what you mean by framing and link this to the story about how different picture frames influence how we see paintings, how we think about them and the value we may put on them. Tell them that when we do this we are reframing our experience.

3 Give one or two examples of reframing and invite the client to do the same in order to check their understanding of the concept. You can use the 'examples of reframing' to amplify the concept for them.

4 Emphasise to them that by selectively *reframing* events in *their* life they can make a powerful personal stress management strategy instantly available to themselves at any time.

5 Take the 'reframing schedule' and ask the client to complete the three columns. Column 1 is the *event* or particular *situation* that they have brought to the stress-counselling session. Make sure they go on to complete columns 2 and 3. Column 2 is the *present frame* of reference they are giving to the event;

column 3 is the *reframe* they will now adopt towards this event or situation when or if it occurs in the future.

6 As far possible, encourage the client to do the whole of this assignment on their own. However, let them know that you are willing to help them if they need your assistance in creating reframes for the events they have described.

7 Ask them to read back to you the present frame (Column 2). Then they can concentrate on their reframing of the event or situation in Column 3.

8 If your help is requested, show the client that you are pleased with their inventions. Take an experimental approach to the reframes and encourage them to generate more than one. Ask which particular reframe they will adopt from the ones they and/or you have created.

9 When the client has selected the reframe they will use with this event or situation, ask them what other situations or events it would be useful for in managing stress for them. If there are others, ask them to make a list.

10 Ask the client to *rehearse using their reframe* for the event or situation they have described in column 1 of the reframing schedule. Be encouraging and make approving comments such as 'That's good. Just being able to see it differently gives you a new frame of reference. Keep doing this and as you do, you will begin to feel differently about it all.' Ensure that they practise the reframing until it feels natural and easy to do.

11 Contract with the client a plan to practise their new art of reframing. Invite them to experiment with more reframing where they feel they need it in their lives, and in any potentially stressful situations in which they may find themselves.

Examples of reframing

Present frame	Reframe
I am in a tunnel and can't see a way out	Every tunnel has an entrance and exit
I am too anxious to study	You need to be anxious enough to concentrate
I know I will never be confident	Being confident starts with having insights about our limits
When they look at me like that, they hate me	People cover up their hurt by putting a scowl on their face
Beggars are criminals and might attack me	Many decent people fall on hard times
She/he is out at night – that means she/he does not love me any more	Private time away can help you to appreciate each other more than before
She/he is so boring, stays in all the time and does not have a mind of his/her own	Easy-going people put others first and are a great port in a storm – a great source of security
He doesn't want to work, he is no good, a layabout, a typical waster – a drain on us all	Lack of jobs has forced good and honest people into unemployment and taken away their belief in themselves

Reframing schedule

1 Event/situation	2 Present frame	3 Reframe

Activity 11 **Linguistic imperatives**

PURPOSE

Helping people to better manage stress and increasing their coping skills involves engaging in conversations with them that are empowering. People bring their own personal history to their stress management, training and counselling sessions.

Indeed, counsellors often ask about the personal history of their clients in the initial or early stress management sessions with them. This personal history, or biography, usually includes significant milestones or life events along the way to the present day. Sometimes it means tracing a particular problem from childhood to adulthood, and how and when it started and why it seems to be continuing as a problem. Typically in stress management the counsellor would be interested in the coping efforts the client has used or is still using to manage their problem or resolve it and the results this has for them in their personal relationships or performance at work.

This approach to personal history is very valuable and has much to commend it. However, what is frequently missed during the taking of a personal history is the rich depth of linguistic expression employed by people and the particular way in which they use language to describe their personal stress-related difficulties.

By paying attention to the linguistic expressions used by clients, the counsellor is able to construct their use of *linguistic imperatives*. Linguistic imperatives are those forms of language that the trainer or counsellor can harness to increase the range of the client's ability to control the stress in their life. The great advantage is that it is the client who provides the essentials of language that form the structure and content on which linguistic imperatives are built; these can then be used to help the client to help themselves.

RESOURCES

Audio recorder
Audio discs
Linguistic imperatives schedule

WHAT TO DO

1 With the help and permission of the client, explore different parts and aspects of their life, their family history, relationships, work or milestones and any problems they may want to tell you about that link to their life.

---

2 Enquire about the attempts the client has made to manage their personal stress problems, what results these have had for them and if they are continuing to manage their stress in the same or different ways.

---

3 Make sure they know that you always want to hear from them in their own words, with their individual ways of expressing their thoughts, fears, hopes and worries as well as their triumphs over their personal circumstances.

4 Ask the client for permission to record what they are saying. Explain that you would like to listen very carefully to what they have to say and that this would be useful in your future sessions together.

5 Record the sessions and then analyse the phrases and ways in which the client describes themselves.

6 From your analysis of the recording, select their most frequently used phrases or words and ways in which they refer to themselves.

7 Introduce these phrases, terms and particular forms of expression into the stress management sessions.

8 Change the form of the expression so as to emphasise the more positive and optimistic aspects of the language used. For example, if someone frequently says, 'I will never get over this problem', introduce the phrase in the stress management session by saying something like, '... and you know there is always a way of getting over this problem'.

9 Study the 'linguistic imperatives schedule' to see how to transform linguistic imperatives into positive messages that can be used to increase the stress management skills of any client.

10 Encourage the client to practise this way of changing the linguistic imperatives and learn to transform them into positive linguistic imperatives that carry a challenging, encouraging, supportive and motivating stress management message.

Linguistic imperatives schedule

Client audio	Linguistic imperative
I can't ...	You know you can ...
It is never ...	And remember you have ...
I won't ...	I believe you will ...
There is no way ...	So when you find a way to ...
I am always ...	There are times when you don't ...
My life is ruined ...	Your life is changing ...
I can't see a future ...	As things get clearer ...
Conflict, it's total conflict ...	You find agreement by ...
I am unable to go on ...	Each step brings brings you nearer ...
It's uproar all the time ...	Just notice a quiet time ...
I could never face ...	You find you face up to ...
I can't let go ...	As you release your ...
It is too hard to bear ...	You learn to soften your ...
I'm stuck forever with ...	You ease yourself out of ...

Activity 12 **The power of self-talk**

PURPOSE

The way we talk to ourselves affects how we feel and what we do. We can talk to ourselves by telling ourselves things inside our heads. This is called 'covert self-talk'. We can also talk to ourselves out loud so that other people, if they happen to be nearby, can hear what we are saying. This is 'overt self-talk'. It is easy to observe overt self-talk in action. However, clients can also be taught to make conscious their covert or internal dialogue in overt self-talk: for example, 'I am thinking "If I am nice to him, he will like me"'; 'Right now in my mind I am thinking that if I say what I mean she will get angry with me'; 'The thought keeps running around in my mind that I will never be free from stress'.

When children first learn to read they often engage in self-talk by reading aloud. When they become more proficient they progress towards covert self-talk, hearing the words inside their heads as they read. When they come across a difficult word children will often revert back to overt self-talk, sounding the word and rehearsing aloud the way they should say it. When it has been mastered they once again go back to covert self-talk.

We can talk to ourselves in many different ways, but there are three ways that are important and fundamental to the field of stress management. We can engage in negative self-talk, neutral self-talk and positive self-talk.

This self-talk can be either covert or overt and it ebbs and flows with the mastery we achieve over the demands we face in any specific situation. The more negative self-talk we produce, the more likely we are to increase our level of stress in the face of significant personal or work demands. The more we engage in neutral or positive self-talk, the more we increase our ability to better manage personal stress and demanding situations.

RESOURCES

Self-talk schedule
Self-talk inventory
Audio recorder

WHAT TO DO

1 Explain the concept of self-talk.

2 Give the example of children learning to read and check that the client understands the difference between covert and overt self-talk.

3 Describe the three forms of self-talk: positive self-talk, neutral self-talk and negative self-talk. Illustrate this by showing the client the examples in the 'self-talk schedule'.

4 Invite them to give some examples of their own positive, neutral and negative self-talk.

5 Ask them to write down these examples or record them.

6 Go over the examples and establish how the client will keep a record of their different kinds of self-talk on the 'self-talk inventory'.

7 If a client also wants to make an audio record, ask them to record their self-talk so they can use it in subsequent stress management sessions.

8 Decide with the client the ways in which they will increase their neutral or positive self-talk. Ask them to keep written and/or audio recordings of these changes and enter them on the self-talk inventory.

9 At each session compare with previous sessions the progress the client has made in improving the use of self-talk and, in turn, improving the management of stress.

10 Help the client to get into the habit of congratulating themselves on any particular successes they achieve through the power of using self-talk to take control of and gain mastery over their personal stress.

Self-talk schedule

Positive	Neutral	Negative
I am able to ...	I wonder if ...	I can't do ...
I can ...	I notice that ...	It's not possible for me to ...
I am good at ...	I assess if ...	I'm hopeless at ...
I am ready to ...	To prepare I ...	I'll never be ready to ....
I see myself doing ...	I gather the facts ...	I can't see me ...
I feel right ...	I have to feel ...	I don't feel right ...
I will say it to ...	Figure out what to say ...	Nothing I say will change it ...
It is going to work ...	How will it work ...?	I can't see it ever working ...
I will start it/end it now ...	To start it/end it I must ...	I am too weak to start it, I am too weak to end it ...
I am in control of ...	To get control of ...	I will always be under their control ...
I am confident that ...	Confidence feels like ...	I can never feel confident ...

Self-talk inventory

Use the self-talk inventory to keep a personal log of your self-talk statements. Pay particular attention to your pattern and notice when you are engaging in positive, neutral or negative self-talk, with whom and in which situations. When you have done this, decide how, where and in what way you will increase your positive self-talk.

Date	Positive	Neutral	Negative

Activity 13 **Stress rehearsal**

PURPOSE

There is a curious and fascinating phenomenon in stress management. Why is it that some people have few problems in coping well in one situation but not in another? And some people may cope well in situations where we do not and yet badly in those where we feel perfectly comfortable. Everyone experiences situations that they feel they can manage without undue stress; they can also identify those situations where they are more vulnerable and likely to suffer stress and tension.

Why is this? Why does it happen? There is a deceptively simple reason. Everyone has an individual behaviour pattern that helps or hinders them in managing personal stress. This pattern is so well rehearsed that it comes into play immediately in situations that are potentially threatening. It is their stress rehearsal pattern. Sometimes it works very well for them and they manage to deal with the demands being made on them. At other times their stress rehearsal behaviour pattern results in stress and only adds to their personal and work-related problems. Improving clients' ability to manage stress means rehearsing new patterns of behaviour that will be more effective in demanding situations.

RESOURCES

Demanding situations inventory
Stress rehearsal schedule
New ways guide

WHAT TO DO

1 Describe the role that stress rehearsal plays in stress management.

2 Explain carefully how stress rehearsal can help or hinder people's ability to manage stress.

3 Outline how stress rehearsal is shaped by our individual behaviour pattern: the way we think, feel and act in any demanding situation.

4 Introduce the 'demanding situations inventory' and invite the client to complete a list of situations that they find demanding and share their results with you.

5 Using the inventory, identify those situations where the client 'is able to cope', 'has difficulty in coping' and 'is unable to cope'.

6 Study and discuss these with the client and then focus on the situations where they need to improve their ability to cope with stress.

7 Select specific demanding situations and ask them to disclose the stress rehearsals that work and those that do not when trying to better manage their stress.

8 Introduce the 'stress rehearsal schedule' at this point and ask the client to record what they think, feel and do that automatically deals with their stress or leads to them experiencing more stress in their lives.

9 Ask them to share and compare with you the best things and the worst things about their stress rehearsal and the personal outcomes it has for them and other people.

10 Encourage the client to construct fresh ways of thinking about demanding situations, the feelings they will have and the actions they will take whenever these demanding situations occur in the future.

11 Support them in spending time rehearsing the new ways of managing stress. Tell them to imagine a new way of rehearsing and managing their stress. As a prompt and guide to get them moving in this direction, ask them to use the 'new ways guide' to managing stress.

12 Ask for a commitment from the client to rehearse their new way of managing stress.

13 Specify exactly where, when and how often they will rehearse their new way of managing stress until it becomes second nature to them.

14 Provide a demonstration of stress rehearsal by taking them through a new way of imagining and thinking about a particular situation, the different feelings to have and the actions that will complement the changed thinking and feelings, to better deal with the demands being made on them.

15 Finish by asking the client to project forward in their mind and imagine themselves in a demanding situation in the future where they are *thinking* in their new ways, *feeling the feelings* they want to have, and *acting* in the ways they say they will. Ask them to rehearse their new way of managing stress until it is clear and they can see it, hear it and feel it in each situation, and hence deal with the stress in a more effective way. Invite them to run through their stress rehearsal(s) as many times as they need to until it 'feels right'.

Demanding situations inventory (1)

List the situations you find demanding and describe how able you are to cope with each of them in turn.

Demanding situations

Description – **able to cope**

Other observations

Name

Date

Demanding situations inventory (2)

List the situations you find demanding and describe how able you are to cope with each of them in turn.

Demanding situations

Description – **difficulty in coping**

Other observations

Name

Date

Demanding situations inventory (3)

List the situations you find demanding and describe how able you are to cope with each of them in turn.

Demanding situations

Description – **unable to cope**

Other observations

Name

Date

Stress rehearsal schedule

	Best things	Worst things	Outcomes
Thinking			
Feeling			
Acting			

New ways guide

Use this guide to rehearse different and more effective ways of managing stress at work or in your personal life. Indicate your *degree of commitment* to making changes and then start rehearsing your new ways of managing stress right away.

	Occasionally							Daily
I will rehearse my new ways of managing stress	0	1	2	3	4	5	6	7

Thinking

I am thinking in a new way. I start saying to myself:

Feeling

I am feeling in a new way. I will allow myself to feel:

Acting

I am acting in a new way. I encourage myself to:

New ways guide (cont.)

Where?	When?	How often?

Activity 14 **Comeback coping**

PURPOSE

We are often able to deal with the stress that significant demands place on us. Sometimes we manage to do this so well that we even enjoy the challenge of coping with stress. At other times we do less well and feel the consequences of inadequate coping or suffer from overwhelming demands made at work or in our personal relationships. There are also those persistent day-to-day demands both at and outside of work that gradually wear us down, so that we have little or no energy left to cope. At these times we often feel unwell, anxious and tired, and our mood can easily become depressed. Such situations can be wounding to us and undermine our will to fight back and overcome any stress we may be experiencing. Often what we need is some inspiration, some belief and some hope that we can make a comeback and begin to recover from the wounding experiences we have undergone.

A metaphor–storytelling approach, combined with drawing and writing, can help clients understand how a comeback can be made. It frequently liberates fresh resources in them, equipping them to better manage their stress. The *comeback* metaphor also enables clients to gain fresh hope in themselves. Using this metaphor encourages them once more to believe that they can make new choices about coping with 'the wounds of stress'.

RESOURCES

Comeback coping story
Comeback coping drawing
Comeback coping letter

WHAT TO DO

1 Explain to the client that they may cope with the demands made on them (a) very well, (b) not so well, or (c) badly.

---

2 Ask what consequences each of these three possibilities has/can have on their health, well-being and thinking, and the way they behave towards other people, and write them up on a flip chart.

---

3 Ask the client to feed back to you their ways of coping well, not so well and badly, and the consequences this has for them and their personal relationships, colleagues and friends.

---

4 Introduce the idea that at some time everyone has, or knows someone who has, made a comeback from damaging stress and this is what we call their 'comeback coping story'.

---

5 Ask the client to write a comeback coping story from the past. Suggest that they emphasise the drama of what happened and how they, or the person they know, made a comeback from stress.

---

6 Read the story aloud to them. This can be done individually or in a group. If in a group, ask the other group members to say what they liked about the person's story and the comeback they made from stress.

7 Repeat the activity, but this time use drawing to illustrate the comeback the client made from stress. Pin their drawing up on the wall or suggest to them that they display it in a conspicuous place at home or work. Another option is to ask them to write up their comeback story in a personal learning journal.

8 Now place the client's comeback coping story and drawing side by side to increase the appreciation of the way the person managed to cope with the stress they faced and how they eventually came through the experience.

9 Ask them to revisit the comeback coping story and select a few special words or phrases that remind them of the comeback from stress. Tell them to write these in big, bold, colourful and 'courageous' script, or word-process them, to endorse the abilities and skills used and the feelings that went with overcoming stress and making a comeback from it.

10 Do the same with the comeback drawing: ask the client to select one or two strong and meaningful images from the drawing and draw them again, only larger and even more vividly than before. They can decide where to place them so they can see them often, for example in the kitchen, on a bedroom wall or at work.

11 Close the session by inviting the client to write themselves a 'comeback coping letter'. The letter should describe the stressors they faced and how well they did in overcoming them.

12 They should describe in detail the personal resources, abilities, skills and strength of personality they discovered in themselves, and also the support received from others, when making their comeback from stress.

13 Instruct the client to write it all down, seal it in an envelope and ask someone to post their comeback letter to them in a week's time. An alternative is for them to word-process their comeback letter and ask someone to email it to them after a period of 7–10 days.

14 When they get their letter or email they should find a quiet place to sit, read it, recall the whole of the comeback coping activity, and remember how well they did in being able to make a comeback from stress and cope so well.

15 Encourage the client to recall what they thought, said and did when they made their comeback from stress, and use the results from this to remind them again of their coping ability in making that comeback.

Comeback coping story

Write your comeback coping story here. Use as many descriptive words, phrases and metaphors as you can to make your story a moving and vivid account of a successful and worthwhile *comeback from stress*.

Comeback coping drawing

Draw your comeback coping picture here. Draw an image or a sequence of cartoons or line drawings that show how you made a personal comeback from a stressful situation. Alternatively, draw a scene or scenes depicting someone you admire who has made a comeback from stress. Put into the drawing anything you like provided it illustrates what you need to learn about making a comeback from stress. It is important not to spend too much time making your drawings 'nice', but it is essential that you portray the comeback coping that managed stress, directly or symbolically, in the drawing(s) you create.

Comeback coping letter

Dear

Date

Yours truly

Activity 15 **SMART stress plans**

PURPOSE

Managing stress works better when we have *plans* that are put into practice whenever we face any significant work or personal demands. Sometimes we are so used to these plans that we think, behave and act automatically. The plans have become part of us; they have become our *habits*. Many of our habits help us to manage stress extremely well. Others create problems for us, such as the habit of excessive consumption of alcohol to manage stress.

The acronym SMART stands for specific, manageable, achievable, realistic, time-focused, all of which are requirements for any successful plan. In developing a SMART plan for managing stress, the client makes an inventory of those habits they wish to maintain and those that need changing, and plans how they will go about putting the changes they want to make into practice.

The key to successful stress management is to choose and create new ways of managing stress and build these into a SMART plan. A SMART plan is useless unless it is acted upon. The client must choose and create their plan and *do it*.

RESOURCES

SMART plan matrix
SMART plan schedule

WHAT TO DO

1 Ask the client what they usually do to manage stress.

2 Invite them to make a statement, either written or spoken, saying whether what they do helps or hinders them in managing stress.

3 Explain that for many people their ways of managing stress have come about through habit and not choice.

4 Explore the idea that choosing actually allows people to *identify their stressors* and *plan better ways to manage* the stress in their private and working lives.

5 Introduce the idea of choosing and making a SMART plan for managing stress. Liken it to a SMART plan in goal setting, for example at work.

6 Give out the 'SMART plan matrix' and discuss the SMART plan for goal setting and the SMART stress plan.

7 Establish with the client that they have a clear understanding of the main points of the SMART plan. Take them through the acronym step by step.

8 Ensure that they make some key observations and record them on their copy of the SMART plan matrix.

9 Invite the client to work on their own (or in pairs if in a group) and complete their 'SMART plan schedule'.

10 Ask for feedback about the SMART plan and what they have learned.

11 Finish by saying to the client,

> Now make a new statement about your SMART stress plan and how it will now be related to the goals you have set out in your SMART plan schedule.
>
> Remember this saying: 'Plan to *do* and *do* your plan.'

Smart plan matrix

SMART plan for goal setting	SMART stress plan
This plan is focused on reaching desired goals	The outcome of this plan is improved management of stress
S = Specific Observations:	S = Stressor
M = Manageable Observations:	M = Motivation
A = Achievable Observations:	A = Actionable
R = Realistic Observations:	R = Rehearsal
T = Time-focused Observations:	T = Transferable

SMART plan schedule

SMART plan goals	SMART stress plan
My specific goal is ...	My stressor(s) is/are ...
To make it manageable I must ...	My motivation level to do this is low/moderate/high/very high (indicate which). To keep my motivation high I will ...
My goal is achievable because ...	I will take action in this way ...
My plan is realistic because ...	To make it a success I will rehearse what I am going to do to manage the stressor(s) by ...
The time I will allow to obtain a result is ...	I will transfer my new ways of managing my stressor(s) into the following life contexts ...
I will review my goals in my SMART plan on (date) ...	I will review my stressors in my SMART stress plan on (date) ...

Activity 16 The higher and lower self

PURPOSE

An interesting development in psychological research has been the discovery that we have more than one self. How can this be so? We behave, think, feel and express ourselves differently in different situations. In this sense, we have a 'situational self', meaning that how we behave depends on the situation in which we find ourselves. To some extent, the situational, or lower, self is dependent on external circumstances; we take them into account and then enact the way we think we should be. Much of the time, the situational self is the one we rely on to cope with demands in our relationships at work and in our private life.

The higher self is sometimes called the 'true' or 'core' self. The higher self consists of our core values and beliefs, and the intrinsic qualities that lie at the centre of our being and form our personality. Unlike the situational self, the higher self is independent of external circumstances. It is belief-driven, meaning that when we use our higher self we deal with each situation not so much as we find it but as we believe it should be managed or resolved.

Being aware of which self they are using to cope with the demands made on them at any one time helps clients to consider whether they are choosing the best way to manage their personal stress.

RESOURCES

Higher and lower self schedule
Higher and lower self inventory

WHAT TO DO

1 Explain that new developments in psychology have shown that we express ourselves in many different ways. Fundamentally, these various 'selves' can be understood as expressions of a higher and a lower self in each of us.

2 Make clear the difference between the higher and lower self and ensure that the clients understand that the higher self is belief-driven and the lower self is situational and depends on the circumstances when determining the particular behaviour they adopt.

3 Ask them to provide examples of the situational self and the core self. Introduce the 'higher and lower self schedule' and invite them to chart their results on it.

4 Encourage the clients to discuss or map out the kinds of relationships or work demands that could be managed well and not so well by the situational self. Now do the same for the core self. Ask them to record the results on the schedule.

5 Invite them to estimate whether they tend to be their situational self or their core self in their relationships at work and in their private life. Ask them to give a percentage estimate between 0% and 100% for each self.

6 Which self works best in managing stress, and why? Why doesn't the other self work so well? Ask each person in turn to respond to these questions to you or the group, or ask clients to work in pairs and feed back their conclusions to the rest of the group.

7 Ask the clients to say if they are predominantly someone who prefers to be their higher or core self, and whether or not this is what they are. Do the same for the lower or situational self.

8 Check this out by distributing the 'higher and lower self inventory' and asking them to complete it on their own or in pairs, using the self-scoring system. Afterwards, find out if there are any surprises. Discuss these and ask the clients to record significant observations about themselves.

9 Encourage the clients to say if they actually engage their preferred self in their day-to-day work or in their personal relationships. If not, what happens? What is the experience of not being their preferred self and how stressful is it, or does it really help them to cope better with the demands they face at work and in their private life? Generally speaking, where people are not their preferred self, they are more likely to experience unwanted stress. Being their preferred self will help them to cope better.

10 Invite the clients to write a final statement beginning, 'I manage stress best when the self I am is …'

Higher and lower self schedule

	Higher self	Lower self
Work		
Personal		

Higher and lower self inventory

Score where you prefer to be your higher self and where you prefer to be your lower self, and to what degree, and discuss why. Score 1 = not at all and 5 = all of the time. Afterwards work through the inventory again, this time scoring how much you actually engage in the use of your higher or lower self in the way that you want to.

Higher or core self	**Prefer**	**Actual**
Work	1 2 3 4 5	1 2 3 4 5
Home	1 2 3 4 5	1 2 3 4 5
Family	1 2 3 4 5	1 2 3 4 5
Friends	1 2 3 4 5	1 2 3 4 5

Lower or situational self	**Prefer**	**Actual**
Work	1 2 3 4 5	1 2 3 4 5
Home	1 2 3 4 5	1 2 3 4 5
Family	1 2 3 4 5	1 2 3 4 5
Friends	1 2 3 4 5	1 2 3 4 5

Activity 17 Job stress/satisfaction

PURPOSE

For people in work, stress is sometimes more related to the job they do than to their life outside of work. Occasionally, we overlook the demands work places on people. The pressures it places on them to perform can range from short, episodic, stressful discomfort to long-term, chronic stress problems. Ignoring this area of stress may even lead to prolonged sickness absence and stress-related illness.

Where there is too much stress at work for too long, personal relationships can suffer. Arguments at home and damaged marriages can result from job stress.

It is important, therefore, to gauge the way people perceive the amount of satisfaction they are getting from their job. Low job satisfaction can be very stressful, and job stress can be considered as one index of low job satisfaction. Therefore, low job satisfaction leads to stress, and stress often results in low job satisfaction.

Exploring job stress/satisfaction with clients helps them to get a clearer understanding of the causes of their stress.

RESOURCE

Job stress/satisfaction scale

WHAT TO DO

1 Make it clear to the client that stress can sometimes arise from the jobs people do as well as from their relationships outside of work.

2 Ask them about their work and get to know something about the job they do. Say something like,

> I wonder what your job feels like to you. Please describe it for me because I don't know anything about your work, and it might help us to get to know each other. Just tell me about it in your own way and in your own time.

3 Talk about the kinds of stress symptoms that the client is experiencing – for example headaches, anxiety, anger, boredom – and ask them to write these down or make some drawings of their symptoms.

4 Introduce the 'job stress/satisfaction scale' and say that completing it will help them to understand some of their stress symptoms. Point out that it is easy to use and that you will be very interested in what the client thinks and how they perceive their job.

5 Explain that the scale is a series of yes/no statements and that they simply need to tick one of these for each statement.

6 The job stress/satisfaction scale is not a timed test, but you should ask the client to complete it as quickly and carefully as they can. They may discuss the statements with you provided this is for clarification only. Do not try to influence the choices they make for any of the items on the scale.

7 Emphasise that, as with other aspects of stress management, the results of the scale and your involvement with the client will be treated in strictest confidence.

8 Examine the results of the job stress/satisfaction scale with the client and then relate these to the scoring guide. Ask them what completing the scale was like for them and what, if anything, they have learned from doing this task. Specific questions to evaluate are:

- How satisfied are you with your job?
- What did doing the job stress/satisfaction scale tell you about your job?
- Is there any connection between your answers and the kinds of stress symptoms you are/have been experiencing? What is it?

Job stress/satisfaction scale

Assessing your job can provide you with useful information about how stressful it is for you. Please respond to each statement by putting a tick in the box if it is true.

Scoring guide Yes = 1 The higher the score the less likelihood of stress at work and greater job satisfaction. A lower score suggests less job satisfaction and more stress at work.

		Yes
1	I find my work is varied and interesting.	☐
2	My workload is not too demanding.	☐
3	I feel my job makes good use of my skills.	☐
4	I am satisfied with my level of responsibility.	☐
5	I do not have to make difficult decisions.	☐
6	I do not have to rush to complete deadlines.	☐
7	I can complete my work in the time available.	☐
8	I am trained for the work I do.	☐
9	I am clear about what is expected of me.	☐
10	I have opportunities for further learning.	☐
11	My work is recognised/praised by others.	☐
12	I am properly rewarded for my work.	☐
13	I can use a complaints procedure if I want to.	☐
14	I am consulted about important changes under consideration in my organisation that may affect the kind of job I do.	☐
15	My working conditions are generally good with regard to heating, lighting, ventilation and noise levels.	☐
Total		☐

Activity 18 Demands and coping profiling

PURPOSE

Many people cope with a wide range of demands being made on them every day. Most of the time they cope sufficiently well with these demands. Stress is not a problem for them in many areas of their lives. If it is bothersome, it is often the case that people regard their experience of stress as not being serious enough to require training, mentoring or counselling help.

Those people who need professional help usually go for stress management or to a stress-counselling clinic for three reasons: (1) the stress they experience is unwanted and in some way disabling, (2) excessive significant demands are being on them, and (3) the personal coping style they have available seems to be ineffective in combating these demands.

It is therefore helpful if clients map out those situations where they can already cope with the personal or work-related demands being made on them as well those where stress is unbearable. This is essential to good stress management and allows counsellors to provide positive feedback to clients as well as identifying with them areas for personal change.

RESOURCE

Demands and coping profile

WHAT TO DO

1 Tell the client that they are going to be considering a useful way of assessing the demands being made on them, the stress they experience and their present methods of coping. Explain that the method is called 'demands and coping profiling'. Point out that it has helped other people in the past and that it may be useful for them.

2 Identify with them those situations where they *can* and *do* cope adequately, or even well, with the daily demands they face.

3 Ask the client to write about or draw pictures of those situations where they cope well.

4 Feed back to them their efforts by saying something like,

> So, each day that you have to face these particular demands, you can cope with them in this way and that is OK for you. Is that right?

Alternatively, ask them to feed back to you in a similar way.

5 Now pinpoint those situations the client faces where they experience unwanted stress.

6 Introduce the 'demands and coping profile' and explain how useful it can be to make an *explicit record* of the demands they face, the coping strategy they adopt and the degree and kind of stress they may experience.

7 Deal with any questions or concerns raised at this stage. Then ask the client to complete the demands and coping profile and decide with them:

(a) the kind of stress that occurs

(b) the specific demands made on them

(c) the coping strategy they use and its consequences.

8 Agree with the clients that they will share the results with you and then receive feedback.

9 Then ask this question:

> Now that you have completed your demands and coping profile, what is its significance for you?

Provided you have permission, keep a written record of what the client says.

10 Complete the session by asking the client *what* they think or feel needs to be changed that would make a difference to the stress they are experiencing. Ask them to take the demands and coping profile home with them, or to a quiet area, and complete it again, but this time to show how they would like it to look in the future at a time when they are experiencing less stress. Review the results with them at a future stress management session.

Demands and coping profile

The demands and coping profile is a useful assessment device to help map out the demands made on you, the way you cope with them and the degree and kind of stress you may be experiencing. Score each situation from 1 to 5 for low or high demands being made on you and from 1 to 5 for the amount of coping you have to use to manage these demands. Also, briefly describe the kinds of coping you use and any stress you may experience.

Section 1

Describe five situations and the demands made on you where *you cope well* and experience little or no stress.

Situation

	Low				High
Demands	1	2	3	4	5
Coping used	1	2	3	4	5

Situation

	Low				High
Demands	1	2	3	4	5
Coping used	1	2	3	4	5

Situation

	Low				High
Demands	1	2	3	4	5
Coping used	1	2	3	4	5

Situation

	Low				High
Demands	1	2	3	4	5
Coping used	1	2	3	4	5

Situation

	Low				High
Demands	1	2	3	4	5
Coping used	1	2	3	4	5

Demands and coping profile (cont.)

Section 2

Now describe five situations where you can identify those demands where *stress is a problem* for you and you may not cope well.

Situation

	Low				High
Demands	1	2	3	4	5
Coping used	1	2	3	4	5

Situation

	Low				High
Demands	1	2	3	4	5
Coping used	1	2	3	4	5

Situation

	Low				High
Demands	1	2	3	4	5
Coping used	1	2	3	4	5

Situation

	Low				High
Demands	1	2	3	4	5
Coping used	1	2	3	4	5

Situation

	Low				High
Demands	1	2	3	4	5
Coping used	1	2	3	4	5

Activity 19 **Emotional reprocessing**

PURPOSE

Stress exerts a strong force on people and their ability to cope. Stress affects the body, the mind and the emotions. Talking about stress often helps to release emotions that have been suppressed for a long time. However, part of the difficulty in stress management is that some people do not know how to talk about their feelings and need a way of doing so.

Emotional reprocessing is a stress management technique that shows people *how* to talk about their personal tensions and feelings and at the same time *creates the conditions* that allow them to release unwanted stress.

Emotional reprocessing is what the name suggests: a trainer- or counsellor-led process whereby clients are shown how to revisit stressful memories and change the feelings they have about past events.

RESOURCE

Stress: my story

WHAT TO DO

1 Explain to the client that stress can strongly influence their physical health, the way they think and how they feel. Put it to them that stress can affect their mind, their body and their emotions.

2 Ask them whether they agree with you and then work together to cite some examples of the effects of stress (for example sweating, shaking, poor concentration and lack of attention, anxiety, outbursts of anger).

3 Invite them to write a list of the kinds of stress they have identified. Then ask them to read it out to you.

4 Ask the client to write down the kinds of stress they have been experiencing and to read them back to you.

5 Discuss the stress items on the list and ask the client to describe in their own words the significance of these stress items to them.

6 If they have difficulty in describing the problems they are experiencing, reassure them by saying something like,

> You are right, you know, sometimes it is very difficult to *talk about stress and let go of your feelings.* You have made a good start.

7 Be sure to emphasise the words in italics in the sentence that invite the person to talk about stress and release their feelings. Tell them that you would like them to help you a bit more by writing their story about memories of stress and that you are really interested in *how* they believe it all came about and *what* has led them to feel the way they do now.

---

8 Say that if it would help them to write their story of personal stress they can use the 'Stress: my story' guide. Introduce the guide and go over the main points with them. The story should be as factual as possible and take a historical approach.

---

9 Although the story should be told in the client's own words, you have the task of:

(a) encouraging them to talk (for example, 'And then what happened?')

(b) showing you are listening ('Yes, I see, mm, please go on, that must have been ...')

(c) helping to focus the client on giving their story a beginning, a middle and an end.

---

10 When the client has written and told their story, thank them and ask them what they are feeling now.

---

11 After they have told you what they are feeling, invite them to feel the feeling, let any emotion come through and then let go. Tell the person to 'just let it happen'. If you think they need reassurance, tell them that they are safe and just to let go of what they can without further distress.

---

12 Let any emotions come and take their course. Stay with the client until they subside. Again, reassure them if required and remember to tell them they are doing some very good work on themselves. Even though it may have been difficult, they have been able to write down and talk about their stress story.

---

13 Thank the client for the commitment they have given in working together with you. Ask them to take the most difficult parts of their stress story and rewrite it to show how it could be different and to describe the different feelings they could have with the different story.

---

14 Ask them how they feel now that they have experienced their stress story in a different way and to describe the feeling to you.

---

15 End the session by asking the client to rewrite, retell and re-experience the different feelings they have, now that they have changed their personal stress story.

Stress: my story

Everyone has their own story about the stress in their life. How it came about and the way they have tried to manage it is individual to each person. Often it helps to tell *your* stress story in *your own special way*. Use this time to write down your own stress story and share it with your trainer or counsellor.

Remember to use your own words and take time to say what you mean and mean what you say.

If you need help to get started, try using these openers:

'It all started when …'

'I would like to begin by …'

'I remember …'

'The story of my stress started when …'

'I don't know where to begin but the first thing I know is …'

'My stress story is like …'

'My stress story starts like this …'

'When I look back …'

'My stress story all began …'

Stress: my story

Signed Date

Activity 20 **Focusing**

PURPOSE

The well-known saying 'every picture tells a story' contains an element of truth that can be helpful to those people who tend to think in pictures or visual images.

Visual focusing can create images or series of visual experiences that may initiate, maintain and prolong unwanted levels of stress. However, the way people use their visual perceptions can also prevent stress and reduce emotional discomfort and personal tension.

Showing the client how their visual perceptions can both create and relieve stress makes it possible for them to practise a form of stress management based on their visual perceptions in their everyday life. By better managing their visual perceptions, clients are empowered to take more control of their lives.

RESOURCES

A selection of relaxing visual prompts such as images found in prints, paintings, photographs, magazines

WHAT TO DO

1 Invite the client to choose a visual image from the selection.

2 Ask them to look carefully at the relaxing image they have selected and invite them to notice the colours, shades and shapes, and the feelings they get from doing so.

3 Ask them to 'really see' their chosen image, to fix it in their mind and to close their eyes, but not until they can reproduce as vividly as possible the relaxing image they have been looking at.

4 When the client can do this, tell them to see their relaxing image with their 'inner eye', with their eyes now closed, and say,

> Really see with your inner eye just how powerful and relaxing that scene is for you and how it grows and strengthens you as you continue to look at it.

5 Embellish this theme by asking them to add any other colours, shapes or images they can see, helping them to relax even more, and to take their time in making that image 'relaxing, comforting and compelling to look at'. Ask them to continue to develop this comforting experience.

6 Encourage the client to continue to create and practise this chosen way of relaxing at least twice a day.

7 Finish the session by saying to them,

> Notice any differences *you* may now be feeling in this relaxed state that *you* can enjoy each time you see *your* chosen image.

Activity 21 **Progressive relaxation**

PURPOSE

Stress can occur quite suddenly or it can build up over a prolonged period of time. However it happens, the muscles of the body become tense in a way that adds to the overall feeling of stress.

Indeed, you will often hear people talking about the stress they experience in terms of feeling tense or having aches and pains in their muscles. This is because stress affects the degree of tension in the muscles of the body. In addition, those people who do not readily express their emotions store up stress in their body.

Managing stress through a progressive relaxation method that involves using many of the muscles in the body is a proven and practicable way to release the unwanted muscle tension associated with stress.

RESOURCE

General relaxation index

WHAT TO DO

1 Find a quiet room where the client will not be disturbed and where they can sit in a comfortable chair or lie on a bed. Make sure the room is not too hot or cold and has good ventilation.

2 Ask the client to loosen any tight clothing and to take their shoes off before showing them how to practise progressive relaxation.

3 Invite them to do a 'mental check' of their body position and to feel how tense or relaxed they are in each group of muscles in their ankles, feet, calves, thighs, pelvic region, back, hands, lower and upper arms, shoulders, neck and head.

4 Show them the 'general relaxation index' and explain that in managing stress it helps to estimate how tense they feel before practising progressive relaxation and compare this with the way they feel afterwards.

5 Ask the client to score their level of tension between 0 and 10. Tell them that the lower their score, the more relaxed they are and the higher their score, the more tense they feel.

6 Take them through the progressive relaxation procedure for 20–30 minutes.

7 Tell them to close their eyes and to concentrate on their feet. Say to them,

Bend your toes and feet away from your body until you feel the tension is 'tight'. Hold it and then let go. Now pause and feel the restful sensation in your toes.

8 Ask the client to bend their toes and feet upwards and towards their body. Say slowly, 'tense, hold and release'. Continue and do the same for the calves, thighs and buttocks.

9 Tell them to tense their fists and then their arms and to notice the feelings of heaviness or warmth and well-being that they become aware of as they release the tension. Remind them to ' tense, hold and then release'.

10 Do the same for the back, neck and face muscles, one group at a time. Tell them to hold each position for as long as it is comfortable to do so.

11 Tell the client to tense all of the muscle groups in their body at once, saying, 'tense, hold and now release'. Then say,

> This time, be really aware of the growing feeling of relaxation spreading through your body and notice that you are allowing yourself to completely relax.

12 Say,

> As you are now learning to relax even more, imagine a purple ball of pulsing energy renewing you and travelling throughout all the areas of your body, refreshing it with such a life force that you feel a sense of complete calmness and oneness with yourself. Stay with this feeling until you become aware of the benefits that it brings and you are bathed in total relaxation.

13 Finally, tell the client that the relaxation session is over and invite them to complete the general relaxation index once more. Arrange some further relaxations sessions and advise them to practise progressive relaxation at work or at home on a regular basis. Remind them to complete the general relaxation index before and after each stress management session.

General relaxation index

Plot and track your level of stress/tension on this 'general relaxation index' *before* and *after* practising progressive relaxation. 0 = no stress at all; 10 = extremely high stress.

Day/date	Before	After
	0 1 2 3 4 5 6 7 8 9 10	0 1 2 3 4 5 6 7 8 9 10
	0 1 2 3 4 5 6 7 8 9 10	0 1 2 3 4 5 6 7 8 9 10
	0 1 2 3 4 5 6 7 8 9 10	0 1 2 3 4 5 6 7 8 9 10
	0 1 2 3 4 5 6 7 8 9 10	0 1 2 3 4 5 6 7 8 9 10
	0 1 2 3 4 5 6 7 8 9 10	0 1 2 3 4 5 6 7 8 9 10
	0 1 2 3 4 5 6 7 8 9 10	0 1 2 3 4 5 6 7 8 9 10
	0 1 2 3 4 5 6 7 8 9 10	0 1 2 3 4 5 6 7 8 9 10
	0 1 2 3 4 5 6 7 8 9 10	0 1 2 3 4 5 6 7 8 9 10
	0 1 2 3 4 5 6 7 8 9 10	0 1 2 3 4 5 6 7 8 9 10
	0 1 2 3 4 5 6 7 8 9 10	0 1 2 3 4 5 6 7 8 9 10
	0 1 2 3 4 5 6 7 8 9 10	0 1 2 3 4 5 6 7 8 9 10
	0 1 2 3 4 5 6 7 8 9 10	0 1 2 3 4 5 6 7 8 9 10
	0 1 2 3 4 5 6 7 8 9 10	0 1 2 3 4 5 6 7 8 9 10
	0 1 2 3 4 5 6 7 8 9 10	0 1 2 3 4 5 6 7 8 9 10
	0 1 2 3 4 5 6 7 8 9 10	0 1 2 3 4 5 6 7 8 9 10
	0 1 2 3 4 5 6 7 8 9 10	0 1 2 3 4 5 6 7 8 9 10
	0 1 2 3 4 5 6 7 8 9 10	0 1 2 3 4 5 6 7 8 9 10
	0 1 2 3 4 5 6 7 8 9 10	0 1 2 3 4 5 6 7 8 9 10
	0 1 2 3 4 5 6 7 8 9 10	0 1 2 3 4 5 6 7 8 9 10
	0 1 2 3 4 5 6 7 8 9 10	0 1 2 3 4 5 6 7 8 9 10
	0 1 2 3 4 5 6 7 8 9 10	0 1 2 3 4 5 6 7 8 9 10

Activity 22 **Stress reduction spot**

PURPOSE

Going on holiday, watching a film or throwing a party all have one thing in common: they are different ways of getting away from the routines of daily life. They fulfil the purpose of transporting us to another place, and in this other place we can relax and enjoy ourselves. We describe these experiences as 'getting out of ourselves' or 'getting away from it all'; we find a place where we can shed the stress of daily working life and pressured relationships.

When people find a place they like or enjoy a particular film, they frequently want to repeat the experience. That is why some people go back to the same holiday resort over and over again. Similarly, they may become engrossed and 'lost' in special moments while watching a film, and in these moments their stress melts away. They may even say that they have a special place they like to visit, see or hear, and fully experience, such is the good feelings they get from this special spot. In stress management terms, this is called a 'stress reduction spot'. Using associative learning techniques developed by psychologists, clients can, at will, rapidly produce their own stress reduction spot.

RESOURCE

Sheet of small circle-shaped blue stickers

WHAT TO DO

1. Explain how, from time to time, we all like to get away from the demands of personal or working life and pressured relationships.

2. Invite the client to produce their own examples of getting away from it all and capture these on a flip chart. Ask for feedback on why they do the things they do.

3. Facilitate discussion about the benefits of getting away, both in our body and our mind, and how doing so helps to reduce stress and promote relaxation.

4. Introduce the idea that we learn to associate certain states such as relaxation with certain people, places and situations. At these times we can even experience feelings of well-being and revitalisation. To coin a phrase, 'we recharge our batteries'. Ask the client to give you some examples of people, places and situations that create a more relaxed state for them and reduce their personal stress.

5. When you have identified people, places and situations, ask them to be even more precise and choose a particular 'spot' that is especially helpful in creating a relaxed state for them.

6 At this point, hand a coloured sticker to the client and say,

> To remind you of this spot, place this sticker on the back of the hand that suits you best as a reminder of your special place, people or situation.

7 Once they have stuck the spot on the back of their hand, say to them,

> Now, just stop for a moment, close your eyes, and become aware of the sounds in the room and the feeling of your body in the chair. As you do so, imagine that special spot now and notice how your breathing begins to be more regular and rhythmical and calming. Do you notice how, as you become more aware of that spot, yes, become even *more aware* of that spot, you are feeling more and more relaxed.

8 Carry on in this way until you can see that the client is more relaxed. You will be able to see this from their body posture, facial muscles and breathing patterns.

9 When it is obvious that they are more relaxed, say to them,

> Continue relaxing in your special place, the place where there is the stress reduction spot. In a few moments I am going to ask you to do something very special, and I don't want you to do this special thing in this special spot until you are ready. So take a few more moments to get ready, and when you are ready and only for a split second, simply look at your hand with the spot on it. See the spot and then close your eyes and after a few seconds open your eyes and look at your special spot again, and then close them and after a few seconds open and close your eyes, looking at your special spot again. When you close your eyes, go back to seeing your special place, people or situation and then keep on opening and closing your eyes, each time becoming more and more connected with your spot, and even more aware of the special place, people or situation until all you can see each time is the round spot on your hand and in your imagination. Finally, close your eyes and keep them closed for a few more moments until you are ready to open them, and come back to the room relaxed, refreshed and reconnected with your stress reduction spot.

10 Issue the client with a sheet of 10 blue stickers and ask them to think about places where they will stick them, in their house, the office and the car. Invite them to look at their stress reduction spots at least 5 to 10 times during the course of a day.

11 Finally, obtain a high level of commitment from the client to engage in back-up stress reduction spot training once or twice a week, using their breathing and visualisation techniques as well as looking at their stress reduction spots.

Activity 23 **Meditating to manage stress**

PURPOSE

Meditating is a proven and practical approach to effective stress management. It exercises the mind and allows the person to engage in 'detached contemplation' of an object or phrase. All meditation requires the meditator to participate in 'dwelling on' on the subject of contemplation. The visual form of meditation, that is, concentrating on an image, is called 'yantra' meditation. When a repeated phrase or word is used in meditation it is called a 'mantra'.

People report many personal benefits from regular meditation. Improved concentration, restful alertness, increased composure, calmness and more self-confidence are all associated with the stress management claims made by people who meditate.

RESOURCES

Candles
Musical scale
'My yantra'
'My mantra'

WHAT TO DO

1 Describe and discuss the benefits of meditation. Explain that meditation is a well-established and proven method of stress management and is widely used throughout the world.

2 Ask the client to describe or draw a time when they felt very relaxed and comfortable with themselves. The important therapeutic point to note here is not the quality of the drawing or the description they give, but whether they choose words or pictures to illustrate their experience of being relaxed and in a comfortable state.

3 Tell them that they will need to find a quiet time at least twice a day to spend 15 minutes practising their meditation.

4 If the client opts to use drawing to describe a time when they felt relaxed, suggest that they try yantra meditation. For yantra meditation they must choose an image such as a candle to focus on. Tell them to gaze at the flame until their eyes naturally want to close.

5 While they do this, ask the client to simply notice any change they observe in the flame or in their thought patterns and just to let their thoughts come and go freely.

6 Suggest that they should maintain the image of the candle flame with eyes either half-closed or completely closed. Let them choose.

7 If the client says that the image disappears, tell them to open their eyes enough to see the details of the candle, any changes in colour, form or shape, and to notice any other qualities such as whether it appears as a dancing flame or a motionless spear of light.

8 Once the image is established, ask them to allow their eyes to relax and close or half close again, continuing to maintain the image of the candle in their mind.

9 The client should practise this meditation for 15 minutes twice a day.

10 For a client who chooses to describe their moment of relaxation in words, suggest they try mantra meditation. Use the musical scale to find a note that they like and feel is harmonious for them. Encourage them to make up a mantra or meditation based on this sound. It may involve words or meaningless sounds. Remind them that they should meditate for at least 15 minutes twice each day, repeating the mantra aloud, but quietly. After the first few sessions they should recite the mantra to themselves internally and frequently as a means of improving their ability to manage stress.

11 Encourage the client to keep a note of how often they do their yantra or mantra meditation and the effects it has on the stress they have been experiencing.

12 Set some follow-up stress management sessions to review how the client is progressing with regular practice at meditating to manage their stress.

My yantra

Date	Time	Comment

My mantra

Date	Time	Comment

Activity 24 The mind–body stretch

PURPOSE

Our bodies are in a state of more or less tension every day. This tension lies in different muscle groups: in our legs, arms, neck, head and shoulders. We also store up muscle tension in our back, hands and fingers.

When we can, we naturally release some of this body tension. Walking, regular exercise and getting up from our desk at work and moving around all help to relieve unwanted tension in our body. However, people do not always have the time or space to release it in these ways. They may be driving in the car or have to complete some task while sitting down for long periods, for example, when working at a computer terminal. This activity shows how clients can become more relaxed in those situations where they need to release tension in their body, but cannot 'walk it off'.

RESOURCE

Mind–body scanner

WHAT TO DO

1 Explain to the client that psychologists have shown how our thoughts can affect the way our body feels.

2 Tell them that right now their body is in a state of muscle tension and this is necessary to support the movements they make such as walking, talking, reaching, leaning, writing and using their hands, for example, when operating a keyboard and mouse on a computer. Mention too that body tension is necessary to maintain their posture and keep them upright. Without it their body would keel over and be incapable of lifting them through their skeleton into a standing position.

3 Point out that too much body tension can lead to discomfort and cramps. In extreme cases unrelieved tension interferes with our thought process and how we feel about ourselves. Excess body tension can also lead to headaches, backaches and bad-tempered relationships with other people.

4 Find out how long the client has to sit at a particular workstation when at work and the amount of time they have available to 'walk off' their body tension. If they do not have frequent and regular breaks and they are experiencing some body tension, then introduce them to the 'mind–body scanner'.

5 Ask the client to sit in a position that they would adopt at a time when excess tension usually occurs, for instance, while working at a PC, answering the telephone or operating machinery.

6 Tell them to close their eyes and become aware of the weight of their body in the chair. Ask them to do a complete check of their body tension from head to toe. While they are doing this, tell them that people find it useful to mentally record the tension in different parts of their body and give it a rating between 1 and 10 where 1 is totally relaxed and 10 is a state of total, rigid tension.

7 Ask them to give you feedback on their ratings and ask them, 'What rating are you getting for your hands?', (then their face, neck, shoulders, arms, back, legs, etc.). Then ask them for a tension rating for the whole of their body.

8 After the client has given their ratings, tell them they can open their eyes. Explain to them that muscles can be thought of as elastic bands. When they are too tense they are like an elastic band that has too much tension in it. Give the client an elastic band and invite them to stretch it so that they make the association between what you are saying and the experience they get from actually stretching the elastic band. Ask them to notice in particular the state of the elastic band when it is allowed to return to its resting position.

9 Ask the client to close their eyes again and travel around their muscle groups in their mind, visualising their muscles as elastic bands and noting the state of tension they are in at present. Tell them that they should see each muscle group slowly and gradually returning to its resting position. Tell them,

> You may find it helpful to feel the growing release of tensions in your body by matching your visualisation of the elastic bands with each outward breath you take and saying to yourself *'relax'*.

10 Ask them to practise this for 10–20 minutes until they are getting a significant benefit from their mind–body stretch. When they are clearly much less tense you can ask them to carry out a second set of ratings for levels of tension in the muscles throughout their body.

11 The second set of ratings should show at least a drop in tension levels in some parts of the body. Congratulate the client on these results. Even if they do not show clear signs of an immediate drop in tension levels, tell them that at least they have made a good start and they can practise this mind–body stretch method of managing stress at any time, at their desk, standing or sitting, and it need only take 10–20 minutes of their time each day.

12 Establish with the client how often they will practise the mind–body stretch to manage their personal stress. Finally, suggest they keep a personal log of their sessions and the results they are achieving, using the 'mind–body scanner', and let you know about any progress they are making using this method of tension control as a form of stress management.

Mind–body scanner

Please scan your body and record your tension ratings between 0 and 10 for each group of muscles you scan. A rating of 0 represents total relaxation, 10 represents rigid muscle tension. Now practise the mind–body stretch. After you have completed it scan your body a second time and rate your tension levels.

Did you experience any changes in body tension?

Toes	0	1	2	3	4	5	6	7	8	9	10
Feet	0	1	2	3	4	5	6	7	8	9	10
Ankles	0	1	2	3	4	5	6	7	8	9	10
Lower legs	0	1	2	3	4	5	6	7	8	9	10
Upper legs	0	1	2	3	4	5	6	7	8	9	10
Pelvis	0	1	2	3	4	5	6	7	8	9	10
Buttocks	0	1	2	3	4	5	6	7	8	9	10
Lower back	0	1	2	3	4	5	6	7	8	9	10
Upper back	0	1	2	3	4	5	6	7	8	9	10
Neck	0	1	2	3	4	5	6	7	8	9	10
Shoulders	0	1	2	3	4	5	6	7	8	9	10
Upper arms	0	1	2	3	4	5	6	7	8	9	10
Lower arms	0	1	2	3	4	5	6	7	8	9	10
Hands	0	1	2	3	4	5	6	7	8	9	10
Face	0	1	2	3	4	5	6	7	8	9	10
Forehead	0	1	2	3	4	5	6	7	8	9	10
Mouth	0	1	2	3	4	5	6	7	8	9	10
Eyes	0	1	2	3	4	5	6	7	8	9	10

Activity 25 Feeding the wolf

PURPOSE

One of the most frequent stress problems people have is being plagued by thoughts that result in unwanted, painful and sometimes crippling feelings that disable them as individuals and in their personal relationships.

Even though people may want to give up their negative thinking, they report being unable to change their thinking patterns. Typically, they fuel their emotional turmoil and misery by persisting in negative, stress-inducing thoughts. 'Feeding the wolf' is a stress management technique I have used to increase clients' awareness of what they are doing, why they are doing it and how they can change their thinking.

'Feeding the wolf' combines story and metaphor with meaning and action to empower the person or group to identify and change their thinking about past and present events.

RESOURCES

'Feeding the wolf' story
'Negative ways I feed the wolf'
'Positive ways I feed the wolf'

WHAT TO DO

1 Hand out a copy of the story 'Feeding the wolf'.

2 Read the story to the client or ask them to read it for themselves and feed back to you what they understand by it.

3 If they have not fully grasped the meaning, explain that when we experience stress, anxiety or depression we often 'feed the wolf' in our mind with negative thoughts.

4 Ask the client to identify any thoughts or memories that result in their experiencing stress and other unwanted feelings.

5 Explain that we often create stress and other unwanted feelings that can be emotionally painful and even disabling, and can affect our physical health.

6 Ask the client to write down the negative thoughts they feed to their wolf on the sheet provided. Invite them to share with you their negative thoughts and how these thoughts induce stress for them.

7 Point out that the opposite can happen and they can also feed the wolf positive thoughts. Give them the sheet 'Positive ways I feed the wolf' and ask them to list some examples of positive thoughts.

8 Tell the client that they can experience joy, happiness, contentment, satisfaction, fun and other good feelings when they feed the wolf in their mind with positive thoughts and memories.

Feeding the wolf

Once a seeker visited a wise man and said,

'My life is miserable, but you seem to be free from all life's troubles. I am tormented by negative thoughts. The more I try to get rid of them, the more persistent and powerful they are and there is nothing I can do to stop the thoughts from getting more control over me, and that makes me feel so anxious and depressed. What can I do? What can I do? What can I do?'

The guru realised the seeker created his own hell because of his pattern of negative thinking. But the guru also understood that simply explaining this to the seeker would not help him solve his self-generated problem. Instead, the guru told the seeker this:

'You know, inside me there are two wolves fighting. One is hurtful, hateful and angry. The other is peaceful, loving and compassionate. The wolves fight with each other, but only one can win.'

What the wise man said aroused the seeker's curiosity and distracted him from his negative state sufficiently for him to ask, 'Which wolf will win, great one?'

'The one I feed,' replied the guru.

Negative ways I feed the wolf

Positive ways I feed the wolf

Activity 26 Overcoming fear and anxiety

PURPOSE

Fear and anxiety often interfere with people's performance by breaking in to disrupt their achievements and goals. A typical example is the person who has a fear of flying, which puts limits on their lifestyle. Fortunately, people can usually identify fearful situations and manage anxiety so that their psychological functioning is not undermined.

Everyone learns to relax and overcome fears and anxiety at their own rate, so do not rush and try to get quick results. Most people benefit from learning coping routines to overcome their fears and anxieties in specific situations, and the activity is designed for this purpose. It is not a suitable activity for anyone suffering from a general anxiety disorder, more pronounced chronic personal difficulties or complex relationship problems.

RESOURCES

Situation fear/anxiety schedule
Threat/fear hierarchy
Threat/fear hierarchy: fear of flying

WHAT TO DO

1 Point out that we all experience fear and anxiety at times. This is usually quite healthy; it is a survival mechanism. It is right that we should fear an oncoming car or be anxious at the sight of someone about to attack us. We would all be filled with fear and anxiety at the prospect of parachuting out of an aeroplane for the first time. These are all cases where these two emotions might be helpful for our survival. Ask the client if they can think of any more. What other circumstances might reasonably be seen as ones where fear and anxiety are necessary? Invite the client to write them on a flip chart.

2 Point out that there are many instances that cannot reasonably be considered as ones to fear or feel anxious about, for example, spiders, the colour red or pinstripe suits. Such items are not intrinsically dangerous. Feeling fearful and anxious about them can be disabling and can paralyse people's functioning and personal effectiveness. Ask the client to name other circumstances that give rise to irrational fear and anxiety. Does just thinking about such things bring them out in a cold sweat?

3 Invite the client to list situations that produce fear and anxiety for them and the stressful effects these have on them and their relationships. Explain that we become 'conditioned' to these situations with a fear/anxiety response. Ask them to write a letter to themselves describing the circumstances that bring about any irrational fear and anxiety they experience.

4 Collate the examples and present them on a flip chart. Invite further comments and discussion.

5 Points to make are:

- Fear and anxiety are not always helpful or necessary for our survival.
- Fear and anxiety are not always rational or based on fact.
- Fear and anxiety are 'conditioned' responses to certain situations.
- Fear and anxiety act against relaxation.
- Fear and anxiety interfere with our performance.
- Fear and anxiety make us look incompetent.
- Fear and anxiety make it difficult for us to achieve personal and relationship goals.
- Fear and anxiety undermine our confidence.

---

6 Explain how fear and anxiety are often natural responses to a hostile environment, but many fears are learned. We can learn to be fearful and anxious about things that are quite neutral or harmless. We can become 'conditioned' to fear and anxiety so that they challenge our health, psychological competence, confidence, motivation and personal effectiveness.

---

7 Introduce the idea that just as we are 'conditioned' to feel fear and anxiety in apparently harmless situations, so we can be 'reconditioned' to overcome fear and anxiety. We can relearn our responses and become able to perform more effectively. Ask the client,

What benefits could you expect from being able to overcome fear and anxiety?
How would you know you were overcoming fear and anxiety?
How would you feel?

Record their responses on a flip chart. Ask them to go back to their list and choose one situation to work on in which they experience significant fear and anxiety.

---

8 Inform the client that they are now ready to practise a stress management procedure that has proved to be successful in helping people overcome specific fears and anxieties.

---

9 Explain that this involves identifying specific situations that produce fear and anxiety and how much fear and anxiety are experienced. They will do this by completing the 'situation fear/anxiety schedule'.

---

10 Invite them to add any other situations or experiences that are not on the schedule.

---

11 With the client, group all of the fear-inducing situations into common themes, for example:

- fear of heights
- fear of losing approval
- fear of losing control
- fear of confined spaces.

12 Invite them to select one item from the list of themes that causes them the most stress.

13 Explain that it is usual to give this a rating of 100. This figure represents the *most* stressful experience they can have and it is called a 'subjective unit of stress' or SUS. It is their SUS score that counts. Everyone has a different SUS score for different situations. For example, their SUS score of 100 might be fear of losing approval of their parents with regard to their boy- or girlfriend. This would be the maximum stress they could experience.

14 Ask the client to imagine a scene, related to the same theme, that is *least* stressful for them, for example, the fact that their boy- or girlfriend lives one mile away and their parents are unlikely to meet them. They would assign 5 SUS units to this situation (minimal stress).

15 The client should do the same for all the in-between situations connected with their boy- or girlfriend: for example, they shop in the same supermarket as the client's parents (10 SUS units), they are coming to collect the client by car (15 SUS units), the client's parents have invited them to dinner (20 SUS units), and so on. They should continue until they have completed the SUS list with a space of 5 SUS units for each item until they get to the 100 SUS units score: fear of their parents' disapproval.

16 Discuss the 'threat/fear hierarchy' and the SUS score column. Make sure that the client understands it and can complete it without difficulty. To make sure there is no misunderstanding, circulate and discuss the 'fear of flying' example.

17 Tell them that they are now ready to practise. The stress management technique used in this activity is called 'systematic desensitisation'. The technique is based on lowering the client's anxiety reaction to the 'weakest' item on the threat/fear hierarchy and keeping their anxiety within bounds as they move up the hierarchy. In other words, they start with the scenario with the lowest SUS score and gradually overcome the fear and anxiety associated with the higher SUS scores.

18 Invite the client to practise systematic relaxation (see Activity 21) until they begin to feel calm and relaxed. They should progressively relax all their main muscle groups and allow relaxation to spread throughout their body.

19 When they are totally relaxed, they should let the first item of their hierarchy come into their mind. Say to them,

> Imagine the scene for 5–10 seconds. Make it as real as you can, using all your powers of awareness to create the theme, colour, touch, smell, sound, and so on. Visualise it as clearly as you can.

20 Say to the client,

> Note any tension you experience from this scene and assign it a SUS value in your mind. Keep a mental note of this for later.

21 Then say,

> Stay with this scene, take a deep breath, and hold it for a count of three. Now release your breath slowly. As you do so, say to yourself, 'I am relaxing ... I feel the tension draining away ... I am relaxed'.

You can also use simpler words and phrases such as 'relaxed, calm, letting go, composed, feeling comfortable', and so on.

22 Ask the client to notice how much their level of tension has decreased. When they have done this, they can switch off the scene and if they want to, they can finish by visualising an especially relaxing place that is associated in their mind with peace, tranquillity and safety.

23 Tell them to repeat this series of steps with the same scene and notice again how much their anxiety level decreases.

24 When they no longer experience any anxiety over the scene they have imagined, they can proceed to the next stage further up their hierarchy.

25 The client should carry on with the same procedure until all or most of the items on the hierarchy are covered. This may take a number of sessions. Each session should last between 15 minutes and an hour.

26 Finally, the client should go back to the 'situation fear/anxiety schedule' and complete it once again. They should observe the improvements they have made and make a particular note of them.

Situation fear/anxiety schedule

The following questionnaire will help you rate your fears. After each item, tick the box that best describes how much you are disturbed by the *situation*.

	Not at all	A little	Much	Very much
Noise of vacuum cleaners	☐	☐	☐	☐
Open wounds	☐	☐	☐	☐
Being alone	☐	☐	☐	☐
Being in a strange place	☐	☐	☐	☐
Loud voices	☐	☐	☐	☐
Dead people	☐	☐	☐	☐
Speaking in public	☐	☐	☐	☐
Crossing streets	☐	☐	☐	☐
People who seem insane	☐	☐	☐	☐
Falling	☐	☐	☐	☐
Automobiles	☐	☐	☐	☐
Being teased	☐	☐	☐	☐
Dentists	☐	☐	☐	☐
Thunder	☐	☐	☐	☐
Sirens	☐	☐	☐	☐
Failure	☐	☐	☐	☐
Entering a room where other people are already seated	☐	☐	☐	☐
High places on land	☐	☐	☐	☐
Looking down from high buildings	☐	☐	☐	☐
Worms	☐	☐	☐	☐
Imaginary creatures	☐	☐	☐	☐
Strangers	☐	☐	☐	☐
Receiving injections	☐	☐	☐	☐

Situation fear/anxiety schedule (cont.)

	Not at all	A little	Much	Very much
Bats	☐	☐	☐	☐
Journeys by train	☐	☐	☐	☐
Journeys by bus	☐	☐	☐	☐
Journeys by car	☐	☐	☐	☐
Feeling angry	☐	☐	☐	☐
People in authority	☐	☐	☐	☐
Flying insects	☐	☐	☐	☐
Seeing other people injected	☐	☐	☐	☐
Sudden noises	☐	☐	☐	☐
Dull weather	☐	☐	☐	☐
Crowds	☐	☐	☐	☐
Large open spaces	☐	☐	☐	☐
Cats	☐	☐	☐	☐
One person bullying another	☐	☐	☐	☐
Tough-looking people	☐	☐	☐	☐
Birds	☐	☐	☐	☐
Sight of deep water	☐	☐	☐	☐
Being watched working	☐	☐	☐	☐
Dead animals	☐	☐	☐	☐
Weapons	☐	☐	☐	☐
Dirt	☐	☐	☐	☐
Crawling insects	☐	☐	☐	☐
Ugly people	☐	☐	☐	☐
Fire	☐	☐	☐	☐
Sick people	☐	☐	☐	☐

Situation fear/anxiety schedule (cont.)

	Not at all	A little	Much	Very much
Dogs	☐	☐	☐	☐
Being criticised	☐	☐	☐	☐
Strange shapes	☐	☐	☐	☐
Being in a lift	☐	☐	☐	☐
Witnessing surgical operations	☐	☐	☐	☐
Angry people	☐	☐	☐	☐
Mice	☐	☐	☐	☐
Human blood	☐	☐	☐	☐
Animal blood	☐	☐	☐	☐
Parting from friends	☐	☐	☐	☐
Enclosed places	☐	☐	☐	☐
Prospect of a surgical operation	☐	☐	☐	☐
Feeling rejected by others	☐	☐	☐	☐
Aeroplanes	☐	☐	☐	☐
Medical odours	☐	☐	☐	☐
Feeling disapproved of	☐	☐	☐	☐
Snakes	☐	☐	☐	☐
Cemeteries	☐	☐	☐	☐
Being ignored	☐	☐	☐	☐
Darkness	☐	☐	☐	☐
Palpitations	☐	☐	☐	☐
Nude men	☐	☐	☐	☐
Nude women	☐	☐	☐	☐
Fighting	☐	☐	☐	☐

Situation fear/anxiety schedule (cont.)

	Not at all	A little	Much	Very much
Doctors	☐	☐	☐	☐
People with deformities	☐	☐	☐	☐
Making mistakes	☐	☐	☐	☐
Looking foolish	☐	☐	☐	☐
Losing control	☐	☐	☐	☐
Fainting	☐	☐	☐	☐
Becoming nauseous	☐	☐	☐	☐
Spiders	☐	☐	☐	☐
Being in charge or responsible for decisions	☐	☐	☐	☐
Sight of knives or sharp objects	☐	☐	☐	☐
Becoming mentally ill	☐	☐	☐	☐
Being with a member of the opposite sex	☐	☐	☐	☐
Taking written tests	☐	☐	☐	☐
Being touched by others	☐	☐	☐	☐
Feeling different from others	☐	☐	☐	☐
A lull in conversation	☐	☐	☐	☐
Other:	☐	☐	☐	☐
	☐	☐	☐	☐
	☐	☐	☐	☐
	☐	☐	☐	☐
	☐	☐	☐	☐
	☐	☐	☐	☐
	☐	☐	☐	☐

Threat/fear hierarchy

Item	Scenario	SUS score (subjective units of stress)
Least threat		Least fear
1		5
2		10
3		15
4		20
5		25
6		30
7		35
8		40
9		45
10		50
11		55
12		60
13		65
14		70
15		75
16		80
17		85
18		90
19		95
20		100
Most threat		Most fear

Threat/fear hierarchy: fear of flying

Item (fear of flying)	Scenario	SUS score (subjective units of stress)
1	Watching a film about the air force	5
2	Attending an air display	10
3	Hearing the sound of a plane flying overhead	15
4	Low flying aircraft	20
5	Reading about air disasters	25
6	Watching a film where there are scenes of planes crashing	30
7	Looking at magazines relevant to flight destinations	35
8	Looking through flight timetables	40
9	Talking about arrangements for flights	45
10	Booking tickets for a flight	50
11	Packing bags before leaving for the airport	55
12	Leaving house to drive to the airport	60
13	Arriving at the airport	65
14	Checking in	70
15	Sitting in the departure lounge waiting to board the plane	75
16	Walking towards the entrance to the plane	80
17	Walking down the aisle inside the plane	85
18	Checking my seat belt in the plane	90
19	The moment of take-off	95
20	The moment just before landing	100

Activity 27 **Controlling anger**

PURPOSE

Anger can be very destructive in our personal lives. Often it can prevent someone from getting along with other people and achieving their goals. But anger can be overcome and controlled. Clients can do this by practising a sequence of steps that will help to 'stress-proof' them from the damaging effects of anger.

RESOURCE

Anger analysis inventory

WHAT TO DO

1 Say to the client that many situations make us angry. Anger can interfere with our performance, particularly our decision making, teamwork and personal relationships, and prevent us achieving our goals. To a greater or lesser degree we all have to face anger in others and ourselves from time to time.

2 So what can be done about our anger? How can the problem be tackled? And what will the benefits be? Either anger controls us or we control anger. When anger spills over into situations that are threatening and run out of control, it is imperative that anger is *not* met with anger.

3 There are several relevant checks that the client can carry out. These form an effective guide to finding out what situations make them angry and how much they control anger or anger controls them. A particularly helpful approach is to map out these situations.

4 Ask the client to complete the 'anger analysis inventory'. They should focus on those questions that tell them about their response in provocative situations. Run through the inventory and show the different stages of completing it.

5 Invite the client to discuss their examples of provocative situations and their responses to them. Sum up their typical responses and the situations that seem to stand out. Ask them:

- How do you feel about these situations?
- How do you feel about your responses?
- What can be done about them?

6 A proven and helpful approach to anger and its control is stress inoculation training, also known as 'stress-proofing'. Stress-proofing involves becoming relaxed and then re-enacting or imagining the provocative situations. Then the next step is to alter our 'internal dialogue', in other words, to talk

to ourselves in such a way that we insulate or inoculate ourselves against the situations we find provocative. The client can practise stress-proofing with this programme.

---

7 The stress-proofing programme has six stages to it. The client should make it part of their weekly practice for dealing with situations they anticipate will be provocative, those situations they find they are reacting to badly, and as a general preparation and practice for overcoming stress and anger. Show them the six stages, using an overhead projector or flip chart:

(a) Present thinking, present behaving

(b) Preparing for provocations

(c) Impact and confrontation

(d) Coping with emotional arousal

(e) Reflecting on provocations

(f) Congratulate yourself on your new thinking and new behaving

Explain the six stages to the client as follows and invite them to practise.

(a) Present thinking, present behaving

To be able to tackle stress and anger successfully, the first thing you need to do is understand your present thinking, the situations that bother you, the anger you experience and the way you behave in trying to manage provocative situations.

(i) List the situations you find provocative, using the anger analysis inventory. Describe those specific situations that trigger your anger. Identify and specify those feelings that go along with your anger.

(ii) Record the way you try to manage these situations. Particularly observe your anger response. Is it rational and appropriate (RA), suppressed anger (SA), anger overflow (AF), or anger that turns to rage (AR)? How do you manage the situations and your feelings?

(iii) Now recall those situations and experiences you have described exactly as they occurred in reality. Record your thoughts, feelings, attitudes and behaviour regarding these situations after you have relived them.

(iv) Summarise your present experience, thinking, feelings and behaviour. How well do you cope in provocative situations? Particularly notice any destructive aspects of your anger. Write all this down.

(b) Preparing for provocations

You are now in a position to specify what you have learned about yourself, your interpretations of situations, those you find provocative, those you react to well and those where your coping is poorly managed. You should be able to tell what makes you angry, what you think when you are angry, how you experience your anger, and the results of your efforts to cope with your anger. You can change the way you react to situations, how you interpret them, and gain some appropriate control over your anger.

Preparing for provocations is the next stage in effective anger control. This is done by changing your 'inner dialogue' or the way you 'talk to yourself', and keeping your general tension level within manageable limits. Close your eyes, let the following thoughts run through your mind and imagine yourself in the situation. 'See' and 'feel' yourself in control.

- This situation usually makes me angry, but it's OK. I know how to cope with it.
- I can work out a plan to handle it.
- I know I can manage this situation.
- I know I can control my anger.
- If I find myself getting upset I know what to do.
- I see my increasing arousal as a sign of energy.
- I use this energy to manage the situation well.
- Provocation is a signal for me to put my plan into action.
- I see this situation as testing my training.
- I believe in myself – just a few deep breaths.
- I've got my sense of humour.
- I'm ready, rational, relaxed and alert.

(c) Impact and confrontation

Once you have completed preparing for provocations, you can move on to how you cope with the impact of situations and how to confront them, keeping your anger under control. Continue to guide your thoughts, feelings and behaviour. Remain in control. This can be done by continuing your inner dialogue.

Carry on reminding yourself:

- I continue to remain calm, composed and alert.
- That's it. Remaining cool like this I stay in control.
- I just allow myself to maintain this perspective.
- I don't have to prove myself. There is no point in losing my cool.
- I stick to my purpose. I won't make more of this than I have to.
- I am on top of this situation.
- I can afford to look for the good points. Little sense in getting heated over the situation.
- I find it unfortunate that they have to act like this. Obviously there is something troubling them.
- I know there is no need to doubt myself. Everything is under control.

(d) Coping with emotional arousal

You are beginning to develop appropriate anger control. This will enhance your coping effectiveness in managing anger and previously provocative situations. You can manage your anger even better by coping with any emotional arousal.

Continue with your inner dialogue along the following lines:

- My muscles are a signal of how relaxed or tense I am.
- If I feel them going tight, this is a signal for relaxation.
- I can keep cool. Just slow down a bit. That's it. Getting upset doesn't help.
- I can see no sense in getting angry. Keep to the point.
- My anger signals what I have to do. I put my plan into action.
- Follow it through. Just talk my way step by step.
- I am not rushed. I will keep my head.
- I reason it out. Yes, I treat the situation with respect.
- We all have a point.
- Bad feeling just leads to more bad feeling. Then the situation gets out of control.
- Even if they get angry, I will keep my cool.
- Now I feel in command. I am in control of the situation.
- My body feels more relaxed.

(e) Reflecting on provocations

When you practise anger control training, you should frequently reflect on the incidents and situations which give rise to anger, conflict and other forms of stress. If the conflict or source of provocation remains, don't blame yourself (or anyone else). Blaming doesn't overcome anger, it only makes matters worse. Blaming, accusations or complaints simply erode your bids to manage anger more effectively. Instead, you should make positive self-statements and corrective comments to yourself. These are infinitely more helpful for managing anger. You should be motivated to think positively and practise these corrective comments:

- I forget about the aggravation. It takes me off my course.
- I don't blame myself. Blaming just makes matters worse. Blaming solves nothing.
- I shake off these provocations. Good – I don't permit them to interfere with my purpose.
- I know practice makes perfect. I practise my plan.
- I feel better. I can think it through for next time.
- Relaxation and control is so much better than letting anger spoil things.
- I'm glad I don't take it personally.
- This way I stay on top of the situation.
- I keep breathing naturally and relax.
- I keep my cool when the heat is on.

(f) Congratulate yourself on your new thinking and new behaviour

When you have been successful in overcoming or defusing a provocative situation you should reward yourself with positive self-statements. Far too many people fail to reward themselves when they have done well in difficult situations. Don't let this happen to you. Failing to reward yourself means you miss an opportunity to reinforce your new thinking and new behaviour, which has produced successful anger control. Failing to reward yourself is a seriously misplaced modesty. Congratulate yourself on your performance. It is the basis of effective anger control. Remember to do it. You should work on adopting these positive self-statements for any situation where you have been effective in achieving appropriate anger control.

Close your eyes and run through these rewarding thoughts. Imagine how good it feels to be able to keep cool when the heat is on. Phrases to use are:

- I really did well that time.
- I managed it well.
- The situation doesn't bother me any more.
- I made it work.
- I did it. It wasn't as difficult as I thought at first.
- I am confident and surprised. It could have been much worse.
- I could have become upset and angry, but I remained cool, calm and composed.
- This way I can control my anger.
- I get the task done. I achieve my purpose.
- I am doing better with this approach.
- Situations don't bother me like they used to.

8 Tell the client that stress-proofing really works, but it is up to them. The more they practise it, the better they will become at making anger work for them and controlling their energy and actions. Ask the client to make a commitment to practise the stress-proofing programme so they get a clear idea of its benefits and how it can be used. Raise any relevant issues in discussion with them. Ask the client to think of a situation where they will put anger control training to work. Then they should follow this up and report on its effectiveness. They should commit themselves to a definite time when they will do this and, if possible, when they will meet with you again to review progress.

Anger analysis inventory (1)

A List the situations you feel are provocative and describe them.

B Circle those situations where you use rational and appropriate methods to assert yourself and deal with your anger.

C Also circle those situations where you suppress anger, anger overflows, anger turns to rage.

Use this key for scoring your inventory:

RA = rational and appropriate

SA = suppressed anger

AF = anger overflows

AR = anger turns to rage

Anger analysis inventory (2)

Situations with my partner that I find provocative

Description of situation	My response to this situation			
1	RA	SA	AF	AR
2	RA	SA	AF	AR
3	RA	SA	AF	AR
4	RA	SA	AF	AR
5	RA	SA	AF	AR

Anger analysis inventory (3)

Situations with my colleagues that I find provocative

Description of situation	My response to this situation
1	RA SA AF AR
2	RA SA AF AR
3	RA SA AF AR
4	RA SA AF AR
5	RA SA AF AR

Anger analysis inventory (4)

Situations with my friends that I find provocative

Description of situation	My response to this situation			
1	RA	SA	AF	AR
2	RA	SA	AF	AR
3	RA	SA	AF	AR
4	RA	SA	AF	AR
5	RA	SA	AF	AR

Anger analysis inventory (5)

Situations with others that I find provocative

Description of situation	My response to this situation
1	RA SA AF AR
2	RA SA AF AR
3	RA SA AF AR
4	RA SA AF AR
5	RA SA AF AR

Activity 28 **Coping networks**

PURPOSE

One reason why stress becomes a problem is that people do not use the management routines that are available to them. This is because:

1 they are unaware that these routines exist

2 they are aware that they exist but fail to use them.

Using coping networks is one way of putting this right and achieving much more control over stress. This activity enables the client to develop and enlarge more appropriate coping networks.

RESOURCE

Coping networks inventory

WHAT TO DO

1 Explain that coping networks are available and accessible sources of support in society and in our range of relationships that increase our capacity for managing stress. Failure to use them may make us more vulnerable to stress.

---

2 Examples of coping networks are:

- family, relatives and friends
- clubs, for example sports, hobbies, social
- societies, for example trade union, environmental, political
- professional bodies.

---

3 Invite the client to complete the 'coping networks inventory'. When they have done so, discuss the variety of coping networks and ask whether they use them:

- frequently
- seldom
- never.

---

4 Establish what consequences this pattern of use has for them and discuss the results.

---

5 Discuss with the client how the kinds of network available to them will bring most benefit when they are consciously engaged to manage stress. By identifying the key networks in their personal and working lives, and engaging with them, they can establish effective 'buffers' that enable them to manage stress. Coping networks also give some protection to their general health and l
a sense of worth and well-being.

Coping networks inventory

Coping networks are facilities and opportunities that are available and accessible within your local community and any organisations you may be involved with, and that increase your capacity for managing stress. Examples of coping networks are families, friends, relatives, clubs, societies and professional bodies. Describe:

1 the range of coping networks available and accessible to you

2 whether you use them frequently, seldom or never

3 the value and consequences they have for you in managing stress.

Coping network	Degree of engagement			
Description	Frequently	Seldom	Never	Consequences

Activity 29 **Life events**

PURPOSE

Sometimes several major events – for example bereavement, divorce, redundancy – occur within six months to a year of each other. These are known as life events and they make demands for adjustment on the individual. Life events impose changes in lifestyle and are often associated with stress and, sometimes, serious illness. The higher the number of such events, the greater the likelihood of stress problems and illness.

RESOURCE

Life events scale

WHAT TO DO

1 Introduce the 'life events scale' and explain how all these events are changes associated with stress.

2 Emphasise that life events can come from many different sources and may cause stress at home and at work.

3 Explain that some events have higher scores than others: for example, death of a spouse = 100, in-law problems = 29.

4 Hand out the 'life events scale' and tell the client to put a tick against all the items that have applied to them during the past six months.

5 They should double-check the items they have ticked and then work out their score.

6 The scale will make the client aware of the demands life events may make on them and show them that the stress they are experiencing is not abnormal. Discuss the findings with them, the significance of their life events, any resultant changes in their lifestyle and the consequences of their score for stress or illness.

Life events scale

Look at each item on the scale in turn and tick those events that have occurred in your life over the past six months. When you have done that add all of the scores and enter the total score in the end section of the scale.

Scoring guide

In excess of 300 points = serious risk, 80%

150–299 points = relatively high risk, 50%

Less than 150 points = low/moderate risk, 30%

Changes in lifestyle	Scale
Death of husband or wife	100
Divorce	73
Marital separation	65
Jail sentence or being institutionalised	63
Death of close member of family	63
Illness or injury	53
Marriage	50
Loss of job	47
Reconciliation with marriage partner	45
Retirement	45
Health problem of close member of family	44
Pregnancy	40
Sex problems	39
Addition to family	39
Major change at work	39
Change of financial status	39
Death of friend	37
Change in line of work	36
Change in number of marital arguments	35
Large mortgage taken out	31

Life events scale (cont.)

Changes in lifestyle	Scale
Mortgage or loan foreclosed	30
Responsibility change	29
Child leaves home	29
In-law problems	29
Personal achievement realised	28
Wife starts or stops work	26
Starting at new school	26
Leaving school	26
Change in living conditions	25
Change in personal habits	24
Trouble with employer	23
Change in working hours	20
Change in residence	20
Change in recreation	19
Change in church activities	19
Change in social activities	18
Small mortgage taken out	17
Change in sleeping habits	16
Change in number of family get-togethers	15
Significant change in eating pattern	15
Holiday	13
Christmas	12
Minor violation of law	11
Total	

Adapted from TH Holmes and RH Rahe (1967) 'The Social Readjustment Rating Scale', *Journal of Psychosomatic Research*, 11, pp213–18

Activity 30 **Stress control breathing**

PURPOSE

Our level of stress in whatever we do is reflected in our breathing. No matter what else we do, we are always breathing. Relaxed breathing is rhythmical and means we are in control. But when our breathing is erratic, irregular or shallow, it means we are tense, anxious and sometimes depressed. Gaining more control over our breathing gives us more control over stress.

RESOURCES

Tension scale
Controlled breathing routine

WHAT TO DO

1 Explain to the client that control over their breathing is essential for control over stress. When they experience unwanted levels of stress the first thing to alter is their breathing and this can have side-effects such as breaks in concentration, distraction and even panic in situations where ideally they need to be cool, calm and competent.

2 Hand out the 'tension scale' and ask the client to estimate their level of tension on a scale of 1 to 10. The higher their score, the more tense they are.

3 Ask them to decide when and where they are going to practise stress control breathing, whether at home, in the office or in some other place.

4 They should also consciously decide how long they will practise the stress control breathing procedure.

5 Hand out the 'controlled breathing routine' and invite the client to practise their stress control breathing.

6 At the end of the session they should again estimate their level of stress on the scale of 1 to 10.

7 Tell them that regularly practising stress control breathing until it becomes completely natural will be very beneficial.

Tension scale

Estimate your level of tension from 1 to 10 and practise the controlled breathing routine for 15–20 minutes. Make a record of where and how often you practise (for example, at the office for 15 minutes or at home for 20 minutes). After the session record your level of tension once again and note the benefits you gain from stress control breathing.

Date/time **Place** **Personal benefit**

Very low **Very high**
Before practice 1 2 3 4 5 6 7 8 9 10
After practice 1 2 3 4 5 6 7 8 9 10

Date/time **Place** **Personal benefit**

Very low **Very high**
Before practice 1 2 3 4 5 6 7 8 9 10
After practice 1 2 3 4 5 6 7 8 9 10

Date/time **Place** **Personal benefit**

Very low **Very high**
Before practice 1 2 3 4 5 6 7 8 9 10
After practice 1 2 3 4 5 6 7 8 9 10

Date/time **Place** **Personal benefit**

Very low **Very high**
Before practice 1 2 3 4 5 6 7 8 9 10
After practice 1 2 3 4 5 6 7 8 9 10

Date/time **Place** **Personal benefit**

Very low **Very high**
Before practice 1 2 3 4 5 6 7 8 9 10
After practice 1 2 3 4 5 6 7 8 9 10

Date/time **Place** **Personal benefit**

Very low **Very high**
Before practice 1 2 3 4 5 6 7 8 9 10
After practice 1 2 3 4 5 6 7 8 9 10

Controlled breathing routine

Step 1 Finding a space

Find a space or quiet corner. You can sit or lie down for this exercise; it can also be carried out in demanding situations such as the workplace as well as at home. Start to concentrate and focus on your breathing.

Step 2 The breathing cycle

Focus on your inhalations and exhalations. Observe the cycles of your breathing. Feel the air filling and being discharged from your nostrils, thorax, lungs and abdomen. Note any cool sensations during inhalations and warm, tranquil effects during the outward breath. Allow the natural cycle of inhalations and exhalations to develop until your breathing becomes even and regular.

Step 3 Regulated breathing – consolidating stress control

As you continue to regulate your breathing, be aware of a sense of calmness, alertness and ready composure spreading throughout your body. Allow this to happen and imagine it radiating through you like healing rays. Observe how regulated your breathing becomes. A sense of balance and control should develop as your breathing cycle is consolidated. You can get some idea of your breathing becoming regulated and consolidated when this 'new' breathing pattern begins to occur without effort. Continue to practise until you can produce the balanced breath and regulated control over inhalations and exhalations. You should find this exercise in breath control helpful as a preventive or remedial procedure for managing stress.

Before doing your controlled breathing routine, record the date and time on the tension scale and circle the number that shows how you feel. Then, after your breathing routine, circle the number that indicates how relaxed you feel.

Practise stress control breathing and keep this relaxation record for a fortnight. Then describe to your health professional how you feel in terms of stress levels.

Activity 31 Benefits versus costs in coping

PURPOSE

Sometimes the coping behaviours we adopt to manage stress do not bring benefits. Sometimes they involve costs. At other times they bring a mixture of benefits and costs: for instance, the relaxation and sociableness that may come from alcohol consumption may also impair our judgement and decision making. Smoking may relax us but will have long-term consequences for our health.

RESOURCE

Benefits versus costs coping schedule

WHAT TO DO

1 Explain to the client that the coping behaviour they adopt can bring a number of benefits in managing stress. Point out that they may, however, also incur 'costs' when they apply certain forms of coping, so it is important for them to identify the typical forms of coping they employ.

2 The client should analyse these coping efforts for the benefits and costs for their health, efficiency, effectiveness and overall performance.

3 Introduce the 'benefits versus costs coping schedule' and ask them to complete it.

4 Discuss the results with the client and ask them to decide on any changes they would like to make in their coping repertoire.

5 Summarise the purpose of identifying and analysing the benefits and costs of adopting specific forms of coping for the client with regard to family life and performance at work. Emphasise the importance of understanding what coping does for them and the changes that can be made.

Benefits versus costs coping schedule

Describe the typical ways of coping you adopt. List briefly the benefits and costs of adopting your specific forms of coping. For instance, consuming alcohol may relax you and this is a benefit. But you may also find your judgement and decision making are impaired; this is a cost to pay for that form of coping.

Specific form of coping	Benefits	Costs
1		
2		
3		
4		
5		
6		
7		
8		
9		
10		

Activity 32 **Improving concentration**

PURPOSE

One of the stress signals that we should look out for and manage better is any lapses in our concentration. Concentration is central to many tasks, for example, in business, study, driving and sports performance. Improving and maintaining our concentration is essential to minimise errors at work and in our personal performance.

RESOURCE

Improving concentration protocol

WHAT TO DO

1 Invite the client to outline any concentration problems they may have experienced.

2 Ask them to describe the lapses in concentration and the consequences these have for them: for example, an increase in errors or accidents.

3 Instruct them to practise the 'improving concentration protocol' for 10–30 minutes each day.

4 Review the benefits of practising the concentration improvement procedure. Ask the client to describe improvements and identify those areas where they should practise further. Suggest that they rehearse, alone or with a group, by reading, imagining and practising the procedure, or by listening through headphones to a tape-recorded version of the procedure.

Improving concentration protocol

Sit down, close your eyes for a minute and then play the following internal dialogue to yourself:

I approach each task with a single beam of concentration. With each task I undertake I approach it with this tremendous ray of concentration. I put out of my mind all other irrelevant thoughts. I concentrate solely on the task at hand. I give it my full and undivided attention.

I find each new task interesting, worthwhile and deserving of my attention. I give it my full attention and I feel the force and energy of rays of concentration directing me on the task. All other things are put out of my mind. Only those aspects that have a bearing on the task are in the beam of concentration.

For each new task I put out of my mind any thought of the previous task so that it does not interfere with my new concentration. I am now concentrating on the present, not the past, not the future, just the present.

The approach I give each task is to concentrate on the task in hand. By being fully in the present I commit all of my concentration to the task. This way, I do not worry or let irrelevant issues or other demands cause me any stress. I am not distracted.

I consider each task as it comes. I find no task dull, boring or uninteresting. I approach each new task with enthusiasm, commitment and understanding. The rays of concentration maximise the use of my time, effort and efficiency.

Activity 33 **Controlling shyness**

PURPOSE

Shyness can be so stressful for some people that it interferes with how they manage significant personal and work relationships. In these situations controlling shyness becomes imperative. Clients can control their shyness by committing themselves to a programme of specific action based on building confidence and positive thinking.

RESOURCES

Lifestyle change guide
Controlling shyness schedule

WHAT TO DO

1 Explain to the client that gaining control over shyness should lead on from a systematic analysis of the causes and effects of shyness.

2 Say that correcting and gaining control over shyness requires them to be committed to a programme for action.

3 Although there are those people who have a sensitive temperament, research suggests that shyness is learned. Tell the client that, just as they have learned to be shy, they can learn to increase their control over shyness.

4 Regular practice in changing their attitudes and behaviour will lead to an increase in their control over shyness.

5 Finish by taking the client through the 'lifestyle change guide' and practise using the 'controlling shyness schedule'.

Lifestyle change guide

Practise repeating the following statements regularly to bring about improvement in your lifestyle and reduce shyness.

A From today I will think about myself positively in the following ways:

B I will stop thinking about my shyness in a negative way. Instead I will think about it like this:

C I will not behave in the way I used to when I was shy. Instead I will make the following changes in my behaviour:

D I will change the way I think people behave towards me. I will no longer feel humiliated or embarrassed. Instead I will think like this:

Controlling shyness schedule

Now put into practice the new thoughts, behaviour, feelings and commitment to how you will respond without shyness. Use this schedule to increase your confidence to overcome shyness.

Find a place where you won't be interrupted and do some relaxation exercises. Then take yourself through this schedule.

I am going deep, deep, deep down into the depths of my mind. What I say and think will affect me all the time – day or night in any situation.

These thoughts and feelings are engraved so deeply in my mind nothing can rub them out. They will remain forever.

I avoid all negative thoughts and feelings of shyness. I easily eliminate those troublesome thoughts and ideas that 'make' me shy. I make myself what I am. I am confident and relaxed. I say what I think and I see myself talking easily to people and listening to what they have to say. The negative thoughts are being washed away like a film of dirt from a TV screen. On the screen is a clear image of me feeling at ease and never embarrassed or shy. I see myself very clearly increasing in energy and confidence.

With every person I meet and in every situation my confidence surges and increases my desire to meet people. I am feeling very positive and I think of all these situations and people in a positive way.

Activity 34 Guiding decisions

PURPOSE

Our minds determine the decisions we make. In other words, we are what we think. When we are under pressure from the demands made on us, we need to find ways to keep the quality of our decisions from being unnecessarily impaired. Mind-guided decision-making procedures help to manage the mind under pressure.

RESOURCE

Guided decision-making procedure

WHAT TO DO

1 Explain to the client that their decisions must be followed by actions if they are to have any impact and lasting effect.

2 Tell them that just as actions should follow from decisions, their decisions flow from the way their mind works to produce them. A cluttered, pressured mind impairs the quality and quantity of the decisions they make.

3 Say to the client that the mind is like a steering wheel that guides the decisions they make.

4 Explain that they can get more control of their 'steering wheel' by using their mind to practise ways in which they can guide their decision making and reduce the interference effects of stress.

5 Share with them that they will find it easier to make good decisions when they are in a relaxed state of mind. They will be able to focus their attention, be selective in their thoughts and attend to appropriate action.

6 Introduce and take the client through the 'guided decision-making procedure'.

7 When the procedure has been completed, obtain feedback from the client and ask them to summarise what they have learned from carrying it out.

Guided decision-making procedure

Guided decision making has four main stages. Practise these and you will increase the quality and quantity of your decision making.

Stage I	Relaxed attention
Stage II	Focused attention
Stage III	Selective attention
Stage IV	Action attention

Stage I Relaxed attention

In this stage you should be relaxed. Use a relaxation method you know already or one from this manual (for example, progressive relaxation). Find a place where you can get into a relaxed state. While you are in this state, talk inwardly and silently to yourself as follows:

In a few minutes – one, five, 10 or 15 minutes – I am going to look through all the information I have that will help me make my decision.

I will be relaxed, calm and comfortable. I will let my mind roam freely over all the information, confident that it will select the salient points for my decision.

I will see clearly the relationship between the essential points and I will consider alternative strategies in my decision making. At this point I will not make a decision. I will simply focus with great clarity on all the relevant issues.

Stage II Focused attention

Now I will go over the material I have amassed. I pay specific attention to any diagrams, charts or maps. I focus on them intently so that I can picture them in my mind. I don't attempt to make a decision at this point either. I simply familiarise myself with the material; I get to know the material in detail.
If there are alternative strategies I begin to become familiar with these as well.

Guided decision-making procedure (cont.)

Stage III Selective attention

I now return to my relaxed state. I imagine that I am making choices from all the information I have identified. I see many possibilities. I just go through the list or lists one item at a time.

When I do this I visualise each one of the possible choices involved and what it means for me personally, what it means for my life, relationships, home, family, friends and people at work. I am positively involved with the range of choices and I see them clearly in my mind's eye. I am also clued in to the kind of feelings that these decisions produce and how they affect me. I consider this for each choice in turn.

Stage IV Action attention

I have reviewed all the possible alternatives. I now see them very clearly. I am clear, composed and comfortable. I am able to look at the range of choices and select one. I select the 'right' choice from the information I have available. Although the situation may change in the future, I make the right choice from the information I have right now. Yet I can see my decisions working out in the future. This helps me to have confidence in making the choice I do. Through my decision I can see the consequences of my choices. Making decisions in this way adds to my skill and competence. I enjoy considering all the information available and being guided by my mind in making decisions.

Activity 35 **Goal management for overcoming stress**

PURPOSE

Sometimes people are far too vague in deciding what they want to achieve. They need to be clearer about the goals they set for themselves and these goals need to be realistic and measurable. By relevant goal setting clients can avoid excessive stress.

RESOURCES

Personal goals checklist
Creative rehearsal procedure

WHAT TO DO

1 Say to the client that although people often achieve the goals they set for themselves, much unnecessary stress is created by setting goals that are unachievable, ambiguous, based on incorrect information, with little meaning for the person and no connection with the future. In short, stress can occur through poor goal setting. This activity will show the client the limitations of poor goal setting and the benefits to be gained by clear and realistic goal setting as a means of managing stress. These benefits require a realistic goal plan for achieving the goals specified. No particular type of personality is more successful at achieving goals than any other. The point to remember in goal setting for managing stress is to develop the skills and practice on well-defined and realistic goals. The client should focus on the correct setting of goals as a means not only of achieving their goals but also of reducing stress.

2 The client should set their own personal goals. When they have completed their 'personal goals checklist', they should go on to practise creative goal setting. Ask them to consider what they have learned and how they will put their goal setting into practice.

3 Tell them to review their progress and pay particular attention to how goal setting adds to or decreases the amount of stress they are experiencing and the impact it has on their performance. They should set a date for each review and the amount of time they will spend on it.

Personal goals checklist

This part of goal setting to manage stress is a simple checklist. Go through it and quickly check off a 'yes' or 'no' answer to the statements.

	Yes	No
My goals are clear and well-defined.	☐	☐
I am realistic about my goals.	☐	☐
My goals are readily achievable.	☐	☐
I base my goals on correct information.	☐	☐
I choose my goals with a view to taking action.	☐	☐
My goals are of particular interest to me.	☐	☐
I keep my goals constantly in mind.	☐	☐
My goals are concerned with reaching future desirable states.	☐	☐
My goals mean a great deal to me.	☐	☐
My goals lead me to make a plan of action.	☐	☐
I practise a plan of action to achieve my goals.	☐	☐
I evaluate and assess the results of my plan.	☐	☐
I assess how near I am to achieving my goals.	☐	☐

Now give your goals and motivation some further thought and then proceed.

Creative rehearsal procedure

Get into a comfortable position and wait until you feel completely relaxed and in a calm state. Practise the following internal dialogue and in your mind's eye see yourself being clear about your goals: they are realistic, achievable and based on correct information, and you are committed to them and will put your plan into practice for future results.

I am clear about my goals. They are well-defined and specific. I see them in my mind's eye and they are realistic. They are achievable.

I have based my goals on correct information, which I have gathered. I have actively set about this and made very clear descriptions of my goals.

They are of extreme interest to me and I am committed to them. I constantly keep them in my mind as they mean a great deal to me.

I also keep them in my mind because they help me with my plan, which I put into practice to bring about the desired goals I want for the future.

I am clear about my goals and being clear makes life less stressful for me. I won't worry about being successful. I am clear about my goals. I act on them and practise them. My goals are realistic and achievable and I do not worry.

Activity 36 **Silencing stress**

PURPOSE

Our busy world is full of noise. The pace can be very exacting and takes its toll on even the most stress-resistant people. But we can do something about it: we can learn to 'silence' stress. The silencing method can be easily used to overcome stress and return to a calm, composed and alert state.

RESOURCE

Silencing stress schedule

WHAT TO DO

1 Discuss with the client the fact that we live in a hectic, noisy world characterised by a fast pace and relentless chatter, and this can undermine people's health and their performance.

2 Explain that this activity involves quietening the mind to become more resistant to noise, pace and chatter. It is about keeping cool and calm when all around are hot and bothered.

3 Tell the client that they should practise silencing stress regularly at least twice a day, morning and evening. They should use the 'silencing stress schedule' each day and regularly review their development using this method.

Silencing stress schedule

Silence is the 'slayer of stress'. Practise this silencing method for overcoming stress and returning refreshed to your performance at home or work. Practise silencing in three steps.

Step 1 Experiencing silence

Adopt a comfortable sitting or lying position.

Now close your eyes. Keep silent for five minutes.

Open your eyes. Describe and share your thoughts and the feelings you have experienced during the past five minutes.

Now ask yourself these questions:

- What attempts did you make to achieve silence?
- How successful were you?
- What was it like?
- What feelings did you have?
- What was going on in your mind?
- What effect did this have on your level of stress?

Step 2 Calming the wandering mind

This step involves 'silencing' your mental meandering.

Now that you are aware of how your mind wanders, go into the silence again. Close your eyes once more. Allow your wandering mind to come to rest. Just let go of the interfering thoughts and feelings. Sense your growing silence and what it reveals about you. Just notice what happens and any effects this may produce.

Step 3 Practising the silencing stress method

Now open your eyes. Note down what you discovered in the silence.

At the end of this activity describe and share the experience. Make a point of observing any benefits practising the silencing method has for reducing stress.

Activity 37 Automatic thinking

PURPOSE

Automatic thinking describes what happens when we immediately link situations and thoughts without any intervening analysis. For example, someone might think, 'My wife is half an hour late. She must have had an accident in the car.' People who jump to conclusions often engage in automatic thinking. They are victims of their own automatic thoughts. Automatic thinking can lead to serious stress problems for people and their personal relationships. Discovering their own pattern of automatic thinking helps clients to begin to take control of personal stress.

RESOURCE

Automatic thinking and stress trigger diary

WHAT TO DO

1 Explain to the client that much of the stress they experience occurs as a result of automatic thinking. Automatic thinking happens so quickly it acts as a stress trigger. Tell them that this activity will help them to 'tune in' to these automatic thoughts and the stress they trigger in their minds and emotions.

2 Point out that a very effective way of keeping track of automatic thinking and its stress triggers is to keep an 'automatic thinking and stress trigger diary'. This will help them to recognise where some intervening analysis would be useful.

3 Ask the client to consider examples of their automatic thinking and stress. They should reflect on the past few days and then start making entries in their diary. They can then report what they found out from doing this exercise.

4 The client should keep an automatic thinking and stress trigger diary on a weekly basis and then evaluate their pattern of stress triggers, automatic thinking and any stress it produces in them. They should note what they have learned and what they can do about changing the stress triggers and automatic thinking that leads to too much stress in their life.

Automatic thinking and stress trigger diary

			Stress experienced			
Date	**Stress trigger**	**Automatic thoughts**	None	Mild	Moderate	Severe

Activity 38 **Thought control**

PURPOSE

Our thoughts influence whether or not we experience stress. Being able to gain greater control over them means we can achieve more control over stress. When we can control our thoughts we can cope better with the demands being made on us at any one time and over time.

RESOURCE

Thought control procedure

WHAT TO DO

1 Discuss with the client the fact that our thoughts guide our every action: the way we are is a result of the way we think. The thoughts we have produce our feelings of stress, elation, happiness or despair. In short, *we are our thoughts*. This activity focuses on how we can be freed from troubling thoughts that undermine our performance.

2 Ask the client to practise this thought control procedure for overcoming stress and managing themselves.

Thought control procedure

Adopt a suitable position and become relaxed. Now lower your eyes and half close them if that is comfortable.

Run this dialogue inside your mind:

I know the ways of dealing with thoughts. I am not a slave to the tyranny of my thoughts.

I am not like a monkey always grabbing for bananas. Never letting go.

I am freeing myself from my thoughts. I deal with them as if watching from a window, seeing all the people come and go.

This is the way I see my thoughts. I can examine them. They come and go. I am free to take action in any way I please. My thoughts don't tie me down.

I am thinking, thinking, thinking clearly and concisely, free and full of energy. I create freedom to control my thoughts, feelings, choices and actions. Stress disappears as my thoughts lose their grip on me. I have control over my thoughts.

I see myself in control. My thoughts are mine and I examine them before I react. I choose to think the way I want to think. I think positively and I am freed from my crippling thoughts. Those thoughts that bother me ... I just let them pass ... like a train in the night. I free myself from stress, for these thoughts are just like yesterday's newspaper: of no further interest. I use my thoughts for me and I am not a slave to my thoughts. I have my choices and my thinking under control and this means I have control over stress. I have control of myself. My control over my thinking allows me to perform well and make stress work for me. I am no longer troubled by my thoughts. I control my thinking, my feelings, choices and actions ...

Activity 39 **Risk and drinking behaviour**

PURPOSE

Drinking alcohol is not a problem; it only becomes a problem when it gets out of control. A practical way to keep drinking under control is to plot the frequency of our alcohol consumption and assess the risk we run from the pattern of our drinking behaviour.

RESOURCES

Drinking log
Drinking risk guidelines

WHAT TO DO

1 Point out that most of the time people don't stop to think about their drinking behaviour. They just do it and mostly it is not a problem.

2 Say to the client that if they have any stress problems associated with their drinking it would be very helpful to plot the frequency of their drinking and interpret this by measuring it against different risk levels.

3 This is done by establishing the number of units of alcohol they have consumed over one week. A unit of alcohol is equal to 10ml or 8gm. Different kinds of drink have the amount of alcohol shown as a percentage on the can or bottle. This is known as the alcohol by volume (ABV) and gives the unit equivalent as well.

4 Ask the client to tell you what they drink and the units for each drink. If they do not know, ask them to look at a can or bottle in the supermarket and read the units for each type of drink. This is important as each drink may have different strengths of alcohol. The units per drink will vary depending on what the client drinks. For example, the number of units in a bottle of whisky is higher than in a can of lager or beer.

5 Ask the client to enter the number of units they consume each week on the 'drinking log' and to interpret them using the 'drinking risk guidelines'.

6 Use the drinking log to discuss their pattern of drinking: where it is heaviest, lowest, most units, least units etc.

7 Compare and share the drinking risk guidelines and the drinking profile emerging out of the drinking log. Look for any excesses, patterns and inconsistencies. Introduce these as material to work on in the stress-counselling sessions. They provide the basis for changing drinking behaviour.

Drinking log

Plot your drinking behaviour for each week and enter the number of units consumed and your risk band, using the categories on the 'drinking risk guidelines'.

Number of units of alcohol consumed per day/week									
Week	Mon	Tues	Wed	Thurs	Fri	Sat	Sun	Total	Risk band
1									
2									
3									
4									
5									
6									
7									
8									
9									
10									

Drinking risk guidelines

Safe limits for drinking: maximum of 21 for men and 14 for women.
Binge drinking: 8 units for men and 6 units for women in any one day.

Units consumed per week		
Men	**Women**	**Risk bands**
1–21	1–14	**1** Low/no risk
22–36	15–24	**2** Moderate risk
37–50	25–35	**3** Moderately high risk
51–95	36–63	**4** High risk
96+	64+	**5** Extremely high risk

The drinking bands are only guides and not scientifically based. However, use them to discuss which band the client thinks they are in as basis for changing their drinking behaviour if it is over the safe limit.

Band 1

Drinking at Band 1 carries no long-term risk to your health. Aim to keep your drinking in Band 1.

Band 2

If you spread out your drinking behaviour over the week you are unlikely to damage your health. However, if you indulge in *bouts* of drinking and get drunk you increase the risks of accidents, injuring yourself and errors in your judgement of events.

Band 3

You are beginning to do yourself and others harm. Your health is likely to be affected and you could get into social and legal difficulties. The most obvious are drink driving offences. Think very carefully about how you will cut down on the frequency of your drinking behaviour.

Drinking risk guidelines (cont.)

Band 4

You are likely to be damaging your physical and mental health. Your social relationships are also likely to suffer. Your liver and stomach may be damaged. You may also experience other problems such as forgetting things and being unable to concentrate as well as you used to. This band of drinking can also begin to interfere with your sex life. Other problems such as getting into debt and drinking and driving will increase.

Band 5

Your physical, mental and sexual health all suffer. You are in danger of causing *serious damage* to your liver, brain, heart and nervous system. Financial and legal problems at work or home and sexual difficulties are also more likely. Other people will be aware of your problems – even though you may not be. Problems in this band of drinking are amplified and multiply. They become more complicated and complex. To make matters worse, you are likely to be dependent on alcohol.

Activity 40 **Alcohol tracking**

PURPOSE

Alcohol itself is not a bad thing, but when drinking gets out of control it can have catastrophic consequences for the individual and their personal relationships. Keeping track of our drinking behaviour helps us to control our alcohol consumption.

RESOURCE

Drinking diary

WHAT TO DO

1 Discuss with the client the fact that sometimes drinking can get out of control. When this happens the costs to people's private and working lives are high.

2 Point out that drinking behaviour can be controlled. The first step in doing so is for the client to 'track' those situations where they have control and those where their drinking behaviour gets out of control.

3 Tell them that the 'drinking diary' method has proved very effective in tracking drinking behaviour.

4 Explain the drinking diary method and how it can be used to the client. They need to look back on the past week and plot their drinking behaviour.

5 When they have done this they will have a clear profile of their drinking habits in different situations. They will be able to spot those situations:

- they can control
- they should avoid
- where they need to practise abstention.

6 Recommend that they use the drinking diary method to establish their drinking behaviour and pattern of control, and decide how they will use it in the future.

Drinking diary

The drinking diary should be filled in like the example you see on this page. Record your daily drinking behaviour or any episode associated with your involvement in alcohol consumption. Use the Comments column to register key points such as whether you 'lost control', succeeded or failed, or if you abstained or should abstain from drinking. Your drinking diary profile can be plotted over days and weeks.

Day	Date	Where	Who present	Outcome	Comments
Mon					
Lunchtime	23.01.11	Rose & Crown	Jean and Dave	Discussed club committee	Disagreement at first
Evening	23.01.11	Home	Chris, Anna, Pat	Dinner	Pleasant evening

Drinking diary (cont.)

Name: Age:

Married/single/separated/divorced Children:

Employed: Position:

Day	Date	Where	Who present	Outcome	Comments
Mon					
Tues					
Wed					
Thurs					
Fri					
Sat					
Sun					

References

Appley MH & Trumbull R (1967) 'On the concept of psychological stress', *Psychological Stress*, Appleton-Century Crofts, New York.

Bills A (1934) 'The relation of stuttering to mental fatigue', *Journal of Experimental Psychology*, 417, pp230–45.

Crawford A (1961) 'Fatigue and driving', *Ergonomics*, 4, pp143–54.

Franklenhauser M (1974) *Man in Technological Society: Stress Adaptation and Tolerance*, Swedish Cabinet Office, Stockholm.

Franklenhauser M (1976) 'Underload and overload in working life: outline of a multidisciplinary approach', *Journal of Human Stress*, 2, pp35–46.

Grinker RR & Spiegel JP (1945) *Men Under Stress*, McGraw-Hill, New York.

Kahn R & Quinn RP (1970) *Role Stress: A Framework for Analysis*, University of Chicago Press, Chicago.

Lazarus R (1966) *Psychological Stress and the Coping Process*, McGraw-Hill, New York.

Oxford University Press (2005) *Oxford Dictionary of English*, 2nd edn, Oxford.

Ruff G & Korchin S (1964) 'Personality characteristics of the Mercury astronauts', Grosser GH, Wechsler H & Greenblatt M, *The Threat of Impending Disaster*, MIT Press, Massachusetts.

Selye H (1956) *The Stress of Life*, McGraw-Hill, New York.

Selye H (1975) Confusion and controversy in the stress field', *Journal of Human Stress*, 1, pp37–44.